Contents

Awakenings of the Absolute Truth are in a bold Italic format.

Further Commentary provided by S. A. Stitz

This book has been compiled for the devout seekers who hunger and struggle to learn the true purpose of life and death by rising beyond their human subjective wisdom to a greater absolute wisdom. Seekers recognize they may never accomplish anything of high spiritual consequence unless they find the key to transcendence. By settling for a life guided by the human conscious mind and its ego, that inevitably leads to suffering and pain is unacceptable. Unveiled within Truth is the path and verifiable awakenings to attract the experiences and knowledge necessary to satisfy and end their hunger.

By defying the accepted conventional wisdom of the human life cycle, the author presents the most challenging theme of this book: identification of the universal form of spiritual existentialism transcending the boundaries of all religions. No mere cultist proclamation, it is presented with detailed instructions for its attainment, and with an articulation of authentic passion. Thus, the testimony of an "eternal energy vessel" mechanism that can be acquired by the means outlined in the text may appear to be somewhat esoteric, but it gains validity when viewed in the context of quantum theory and Jung's theory on the collective unconscious.

The awakenings revealed unveil, explain, and diagram Universal Nature's absolute, essential, and verifiable spiritual path to Pure Mind that awakens Absolute Truth and its vehicle that empowers perpetual reincarnations. It is a discipline inspired and driven by Universal Nature so that humankind may transcend appearances and penetrate to the very source of all wisdom.

The path to Pure Mind and its spiritual awakenings have existed infinitely, giving humans the one chance to effectuate their true-life purpose. Spiritual awakenings are not the final destination. They are the engine to reach clear insight and awareness, to be used and manifested, not just collected.

The fulfillment of our True Nature is a matter of becoming

FORWARD

It is because man's mind and overpowering desire craves to learn that which can be verified to be greater and more fruitful than the current dogmas that religiously guide his subjective reality into a state of mental chaos that the undisputable Truth is unveiled. With his lack of knowledge concerning the fundamental nature, the purpose of his being, and the Nature of Existence that encompasses it, he suffers.

Deficient in his awareness of that which exists but cannot be seen, he ponders a myriad of questions. Finding that the answers being offered have been presented with no proof toward reality or to have ever even existed. His "hungry ghost" that longs for Truth remains unfulfilled.

Now that humanity and this planet that he inhabits has fallen into a state of chaos it is time man heeds the laws of Universal Nature. Awakened Beings have spoken, but you have not listened. They spoke to you while in human form, they spoke to you through numerous languages, they spoke to you by means of the various art forms, they spoke to you with cave paintings, they spoke to you with impossible human feats, they spoke to you with hieroglyphics, and you are warned by "natural disasters", and the disasters that you yourselves have created.

Awakened Beings have spoken to you of love, peace, and the oneness of all living things. You responded with ego emotion, hate, war, killing, pestilence, torture, industrial and chemical waste. Nature gave you a planet with beautiful flora and fauna, and creatures to inhabit it. Yet you have set a path of destruction of all that exists on this planet.

Awakened Beings have spoken to humanity throughout the ages, but man has not heeded what has been said.

In the following pages, we will attempt once more, most likely for the final time, to lay aside false realities and myths, so that the Truth of all Existence and its purpose will guide your thinking and actions.

EMERGING

Because man is in the embryonic stage of his evolution, he continues to be haunted by a "hungry ghost," which resides in all human beings. This presence is manifested in a human's longing to fill the emptiness created by his unanswered yet endless search for Absolute Truth, defined as; Truth that cannot be changed by the mind or deceptions of man. Consequently, it is impossible to quench this ravenous thirst by performing any logical, emotional, or physical activity that stems from his human desires.

To put an end to this endless longing and restlessness, man must go beyond his conscious mind and reach out to the spiritual dimensions. It is there they will experience the true nature and reason for his hungry ghost.

A human's hungry ghost exists for them to be made aware of the necessity to awaken the answer of why they exist. In order to comprehend with crystal clarity, the answer they must also learn the why, who, and what of all phenomena. This can only be achieved by awakening to the essence of Existence.

The hungry ghost we speak of is not the same hungry ghost Buddhists address in their dialogue concerning the human condition of craving or desire. The hunger they speak of stems from the nature of the human species. This species being a singular part of the higher Nature of Existence also carries with it the ravenous desire to know itself. This desire translates into man's profound need to fulfill his ultimate reason for being, and that is the hungry ghost of which we speak. Again, in order to quench this thirst for Truth man must travel beyond himself and awaken to his true Self.

My meditation: In this world of ego and suffering I seek to melt into a state where I escape the meaningless activity of my conscious mind. In beautiful isolation I seek aloneness and silence; it is here I am afforded a glimpse of the reality of Existence; a glimpse of the simple yet pure Truth.

Following the true Path will afford the human the ability to see clearly through eyes that are not clouded by misconception, delusion, misbelief, and personal ego. A direct Path accomplishes this by leading them through a transcendence of their human mind and ego and places them at a point beyond their ego self and they become an objective spectator of all physical and spiritual evolutionary causes and events.

Therefore, a life of spiritual preparation is the only life worth living for it leads to the fulfillment of humanity's purpose.

Although there are many so-called spiritual schemes and religions in practice today, they are virtually all devoid of a meaningful value. When studied with curiosity towards their practicality of spiritual attainment and awakening, they only prove to serve and/or satisfy personal, religious, and communal sentiment and emotional needs. This proves to be true no matter what their definitions of spiritual matters may be.

Throughout the years of devotion to formal and non-formal religions and sects' true fervent devotees found only wounded egos, and heartfelt frustration created by a lack of high spiritual attainment and has inevitably discarded these disciplines. Some of these same disciplines are still being preached and practiced today by unenlightened beings who for the most part seek only relief from their personal failings and/or financial gain from those who seek Truth.

Awakening experiences come when the conscious mind is set aside, and the spiritual dimensions are reached. They do not, nor cannot come from religious doctrine, cultural dictates, or the logical mind. Truth cannot be learned from conferences, workshops, or books. Man's embodiment of Truth is an ongoing culmination of awakenings formed by experience and clear perception, not a parroting of words and/or rituals. Man learns directly from awakening experiences achieved by developing the correct mechanisms rather than imitating tradition. This leads to the embodiment and integrity of Truth that is attained by an uncluttered personal relationship with Existence.

Students of the true Pathway are willing participants in the realm of learning in order to reach the highest spiritual levels, thereby ending the separation created by the conscious mind and ego illusions. Steps along the Path face risks, a need for patience, and most importantly a surrender of man's ego desires.

Knowledge is not the final destination on man's journey. It is one of the tools to reach clear insight, awareness, and oneness. Knowledge is to be used not collected.

The true Pathway to awakening guided and driven by the Nature of Existence (the building blocks [DNA] of all phenomena) and by its alignment with the oneness of all phenomena proves to be the veritable Path beyond this human condition resulting in awakening to the indisputable Absolute Truths that man has sought throughout the ages.

TRUTH

ABSOLUTE TRUTH: *Awakened Truths are not formulated beliefs as can be seen in most religions but are recognized and known as Absolute. They come directly from enlightened communication by means of the highest spiritual dimensions.*

...a supreme entity or being can only be described as Existence itself.

...Existence transcends form, space, and time.

...Existence has no origin, no ending, no self, no face, no emotion, and no direction.

...Everything that exists is existent within Existence.

...Existence is the only phenomena that does not depend upon other things for its existence.

...Existence is energy.

...If man allows Existence's energy to flow purposelessly throughout his life then his life has no meaning.

...The fulfillment of man's true nature is a matter of becoming, not just a matter of being.

...It is for each humanoid to transcend his human nature and condition to become an Eternal Being; A Being of In-Perpetuum energy.

...Existence's Immanent Nature is pure consciousness that flows through all forms and space as energy, and as such is known as the Breath of Existence. It is this power that guides and dictates the creation of and the natural essence of all phenomena's existence.

...the Breath of Existence is the energy that encompasses, transports, and communicates the essence of Itself, which is the essence of all Truth and wisdom that man awakens by following the Pure Mind Path and through deep meditation and various other disciplines.

...Existence's Nature, residing in silence, is the nature beyond all

other natures including human nature. It permeates all phenomena as their sole and ultimate authority.

...the direct Path named Pure Mind is the veritable and verifiable way leading beyond the ignorance of the human's conditioned mind to enlightenment, and the eternal state of In-Perpetuum.

...awakened enlightenment proves absolutely useless unless manifested in a moral atmosphere of sensitivity as defined by Nature's Law.

...all life is rooted in the One Existence with its own Nature that flows as energy into the twelve spiritual and three physical dimensions of consciousness.

...the Path of Pure Mind is the instrument humanity is given to awaken the truth of the One Existence, the Nature of that Existence, and the Breath of Existence's Truth.

...beings in an In-Perpetuum state travel between physical and spiritual planes virtually simultaneously; they are the activity of Existence and reality themselves.

...the Law of cause and effect (karma) carries with it the reverse side of no-cause/no-effect. The state of man's eternal life is an effect, and the Path of Pure Mind is the cause. (Reincarnation is not an automatic event; it must be attained, and vigorously maintained.)

...beyond unevolved human nature there is no intrinsic evil, no basis for fear, no separation ego, no frustration, no human desire, no expectation, therefore no suffering.

To understand the wayward man, you must study man's corrupt manipulation of Truths throughout the ages. The Ultimate Truth of Existence was bastardized into a relative truth of an emotional supreme being having the appearance of man. Attaining Existence's high state of an In-Perpetuum Being became many things throughout the ages for example: an involuntary reincarnation by some, earning a seat in heaven alongside God by others, etc., all to explain what religious organizations could not explain nor could they achieve.

The greatest corruption is that of God itself. The Absolute Truth is:

Existence itself always was and always will be; there can never be non-existence of existence. This is in opposition to all other states that exist only in a timeframe, and until energized they were only latent possibilities that resided within existence itself. All forms or thoughts that exist reach a point of nonexistence, and therefore, you can say that those things either will exist or have existed. And in what category would you put God? If you say he exists, he will reach a non-existent state and is therefore not eternal.

PASSAGE

The Path to Pure Mind is a spiritual practice enabling one to evolve, manifesting through the purification of energy into the perpetual state of being/nonbeing. This comprises the integration of awakenings and the embodiment of those awakenings; together they will bring into focus the Nature of Existence. The Path places mind and body in the right motion around a sphere that has four main directions of energy creation and flow. They are downward flow, created by knowledge or understanding; inward flow, created by meditation; outward flow, created by the manifestation of awakenings; and upward flow, created by awakening or enlightenment.

There can be absolutely no gain to be had unless the Path is lived in an atmosphere comprising the positive emotions of sensitivity and kindness practiced in a moral way. Morality is conduct that is set forth by Existence's Laws of Nature which resides beyond human nature as well as the natures of all other living things. Morality's characteristics of conduct are a binding force that helps hold together the positive energy which we strive to create.

When practiced with great intensity this Path produces enough purified perpetual energy to enable a practitioner to totally liberate his energy vessel from mind/body and further to evolve into the state of In-Perpetuum whose primary purpose is the creation of all phenomena. Other than being described as being in perpetual forms, he can also be described as having the qualities of being/nonbeing, thought/non-thought, dimension/non-dimension, timelessness, as well as spacelessness, etc.

The awakening experiences created while on the Path are a totally personal affair. It is mandatory to understand that success in attaining liberation, though dependent solely on one's own efforts, may also require an awakened reincarnates guidance to make it all possible. When awakenings occur on the Path to a Pure Mind, the practitioner evolves to embody those awakenings. Awakenings that do not become part of one's living practice are in fact not awakenings at all and therefore are totally useless.

False seekers are usually identified by their unwillingness to undergo the rigors of a deep practice. If a person is not willing to get to know himself through this simple method, such as meditation, the attempt of more advanced methods will place him in peril. Actually, it is better if he avoids all other physical attempts rather than allow himself to be influenced by energies that will magnify his fears and faults. If it were to be said that Zen practice has a golden truth, it would be its ability to help one understand one's self in order to cure his fears and faults. This removes his ego-driven emotions so that they are not involved in advanced spiritual practice. It can also bring with it an effective way of approaching the Path to Pure Mind and Its advanced practice.

We invariably use the term "walking the Path," but it is only a metaphor for embodying the circular Path. "Actually, neither you nor the Path moves; it is only your mind that moves."When you understand this phrase, you will know that you have started on the right Path.

It has been said that the Path to Pure Mind places a great deal of emphasis on meditation, mindfulness, and contemplation, but these three channels, though inseparable from each other, form only one piece of the circle. Together they lead to enlightened awakenings, which are another part of the circle; these awakenings can only be verified by true understanding, and further, they must be manifested by the fourth direction of the circle, by living and being the awakenings.

It is a great mistake to judge the Path to Pure Mind, its forms and techniques, as being the same as what is being practiced in other disciplines. Outward appearances are not reality.

It has been and will continue to be proven by its rate of successful transcendence that the Path to Pure Mind will accomplish more towards awakening than the practice of Buddhism, Zen, Hindu, or other modern new age techniques. The fact is that you can reach states of joy and bliss with Hindu meditations, a state of calmness with Buddhist methods, and ability to function well in the world under Zen guidance, and possibly even gain relief from symptoms mental and physical that modern Western medicine can't cure. But all these states or gains are illusory when compared to the immortal state reached by transcending the human condition.

The Path to Pure Mind is timeless; transcending all forms and is the way as proven by it allowing you to experience Truth. The primary difference of Pure Mind is that with the other practices you learn about things seen as scholastic knowledge, and you learn of it seen as subjective knowledge. With Pure Mind, you learn in and through it, and it is seen as inner perception.

The about and of things are just more layers of knowledge, but through the Path to Pure Mind you can be permanently transformed. Restlessness in the practitioners of all other forms of spiritual disciplines arises as they get a glimpse of something they are trying to reach, but it cannot be attained with these other schools.

Traditional wisdom employed by many religions with their elaborate isolation techniques both long term called monasticism or short term such as seven-day retreats etc. are only a process of conditioning to cement and reflect shallow practices and provoke mental and physical refuge.

Buddhism in total and Hinduism in part treat meditation solely as a device to make you aware of your real Self which is not created by you, but which you already are, and therefore you need not to create anything. With the Path to Pure Mind you become aware of the need to create and bind pure energies in order to become perpetual. Creation of this sort is the first step towards becoming a "creator" of future phenomena.

A highly honed practice of acute awareness is a very important skill and encompasses more than just a momentary noticing of an event or thought. It is the vital and controlling vehicle which puts us in touch with the Breath of Existence and the energy of all things. It is the bridge between normal material reality and spiritual reality. This is a skill we are born with but in a culture stressing strict logic to explain everything in the physical universe this skill is forgotten and lost to most.

Children in their attempt to master the physical and cultural ways of life, slowly but surely close their door to the spiritual world. Yes, to a certain degree this is necessary so that they may know the difference between the physical and the spiritual worlds.

Much later in the human evolution people will focus on the physical world without becoming attached to it. Not getting lost in their memory progression, they will be able to go between both the physical and spiritual dimensions without losing touch of either. But until that time the building of the bridge to the unknown requires a practitioner to live a moral life and to practice a true meditation technique to accomplish this feat.

Acute awareness and a high state of mindfulness are required for the attraction and transference of pure energy, and that is man's aim. When reaching the meditative state which allows awakening, one must first know that only the mind which is receptive, here and now, can create this meditative state. Rigidity creates tension, and a tense mind can never be receptive or meditative. The practitioner, therefore, must remain relaxed/weightless and in a non-doing state.

Probably the most important thing is to go beyond the paradox of meditation as being the end result. Even though our meditations are extremely important, used by us for many critical happenings, we must approach meditation as such; an end to itself. Only then can the results we seek be attained. It is said you must learn and understand good meditation techniques.

In the ultimate sense, meditation is not technique; it is acute awareness. When the right techniques are used, growth explodes. Otherwise, you just wander and search and gained nothing. At the beginning meditation seems to be something one does or is doing, but when one is able to reach a deep state the doing disappears. The same can be said which applies to effort.

With success, effort disappears, and it's all spontaneous and effortless. You go beyond, you're just there, acutely aware, and it happens. You sit, you dance, and you walk, whatever technique you are in, it just happens. With practice, you will be capable of leaving effort behind and beginning your inner transformation.

Our minds are intricate, complex, and delicate. If you don't know or understand what to do it is much better to do nothing because whatever you do that's wrong creates more problems that it can solve. Don't start unless you fully understand or have a Pure Mind teacher guiding you. Try never to mix two or a more techniques, because their functions can be totally different. Sometimes they may even be diametrically opposed. Don't change or try to improve what has been proven successful since the beginning of time. When you don't understand or know, non-doing can be more beneficial.

Existence's nature is truth as the Path to Pure Mind is the embodiment of that truth. An ordinary mind cannot fully understand these truths nor can awakened enlightenment be successfully communicated verbally.

If, as with most people, you find that you cannot bring yourself to practice, at least try to understand the nature of your hungry ghost and live by Existence's law of moral codes in your everyday life ultimately giving that life a meaningful existence.

EXISTENCE

Anything is possible when people set out to reach beyond their logical minds to the spiritual realm. What is impossible is thinking that they can make the rules or set the regimen.

Existence's Pure Mind practice of mindful living creates awareness. It is the living practice that helps fulfill Existence's Nature and thereby man's nature and his reason for being.

Existence's Pure Mind's living practice must be approached as a coherent whole, not as a way of life that can be co-mingled with pre-existing ideologies.

The problem for most seekers is that they bring with them their culture, religious environment, educational tools, and the need to understand things in a logical way. They thereby view this most spiritual of practices in a conditioned manner. Unfortunately, most Western seekers accept influence by this practice only when a great many of the words and ideas fall in line with their previously accepted ideologies. They tend to respond to symbols, labels, and titles. It is very difficult for them to realize that true teachers do not acknowledge certain so-called sacramental, spiritual idols and concepts. These seekers also hold a vast range of assumptions and use a great deal of imagination about what is spiritual and what is not.

What was at one time highly effective spiritual practices are today watered-down approximations with meaningless ritual instruments and words. Those who practice these exoteric religions demonstrate by their actions the lack of true inner faith and understanding. Because of modern-day superficial and shallow paths to practice, most seekers do not know how to approach a teacher and teaching as a whole entity. In addition, they failed to understand that they must prepare with the intensity that comes from deep self-searching motivated by their hungry ghost before they can attract a true guide for their spiritual practice. The mystical Islamists use the term collectors of trifles for those who seek teachings which fit comfortably in with their accepted pattern or that embody various parts of other teachings which also fit into their ideas of truth or spirituality.

One of the most important qualities in a prospective student is his ability and desire to be powerfully influenced without asking why or how it is so.

Humans generally have the commanding desirous ego which needs to control what they believe, or at the least choose what to accept. This is their ego need to protect all the relative truths of their systems and in turn garner some meaning for their lives. Unfortunately, most religions or systems on this planet heavily condition people, and because man does not like to think of himself as conditioned, he says things like "we are dedicated" or "very religious," and they live with that explanation. But their minds are engineered to believe whatever the system asks.

Man, as a newborn child, has but a few veils; therefore, he is in constant contact with the spiritual dimensions; consequently Existence's Nature is man's natural system of belief with no questions left to be asked.

One of man's greatest obsessions is to question everything in order to understand things logically, and only when our logical minds are satisfied with something's validity will we accept it as certainty. This is not a posture that lends itself to learning, because it sets preconditions, which greatly limits our ability to go beyond rationality into spiritual dimensions. If you bring certainty as a commanding principle for learning, you bring often tried, failed, and rejected methods, and you will never learn the essence of what "is." The other obsession which is a great hindrance is habit patterns, a form of self-conditioning. Both of these conditions can be bypassed when one goes beyond human nature and awakens to one's true self-image and then embodies that reflection. In other words, you are embodying the true self and not imitating other people or becoming what they expect. *Enlightenment eliminates misconception.*

There are four principal channels or directions on the living Path; each having the primary function of creating pure cohesive energy. There are also many secondary channels, but all have the end result of energy production with the difference being in the amount, strength, and polarity. Do not speak of steps along your Path, only think in terms of breaths. With each breath, you take in each and every moment, seek to awaken Truth. Existence's truth is in opposition to most religions and their spiritual beliefs. Life is not and should not remain a mystery. The mission of humanity is to awaken and embody those awakenings in one's everyday life. EXISTENCE IS ENERGY, AND IF IT FLOWS PURPOSELESSLY, THEN ALL LIFE HAS NO WORTH. The very act of existing is not an achievement. Its intrinsic values lie in creation, experiencing, and awakening. These events are also the intrinsic values of the circle of life.

In a high spiritual meditative state, you experience the purpose of life. It is at this point that life becomes freer, free from the mysteries that plague the human, free from the question of life and death, free from the uncertainties of good and evil, and free from the boundaries of the human suffering condition.

Reaching this point awakened beings begin to lighten up and truly enjoy their lives. They can laugh, sing, and dance for no apparent reason. Their weights have been lifted, and they understand that they cannot be judged by the unenlightened masses, and so we find the real meaning of that "crazy monk living on the hill."

Spirituality unadorned is the difference. It is the deep inner search that leads to awakening and the embodiment of those awakenings. Existence's Nature and therefore it's true Path to Pure Mind asks nothing from practitioners but a relationship of trust, and a willingness to allow awakenings to work. Universal Nature's relationship with the practitioner is one of intimate love, powerful inspiration, and great trust. If the seeker is unwilling in any facet of the relationship, then his ego is in play, and it all turns to nonsense. The transformation of a practitioner to an awakened being comes with his willingness to surrender and giving his complete trust unconditionally.

It is at this point that we reach the crux of practice and attainment, for the act of surrender is a very decisive step. It is not just a matter of faith in a Path or a God, but true faith in oneself.

I recognize the act of surrender is a touchy subject with many ambiguous implications. Most people, especially those from Western cultures have no background or understanding of the relationship between a guide and a student. True faith in one spiritual practice and its guide demands total trust. This in no way conflicts with statements of accepting only your own awakening experiences as truth. Without surrender to a Path, those deep awakenings will never arise. Those who have experience in awakening might more easily understand.

Surrender cannot take place unless the seeker has total confidence in his decision to do so. A seeker or practitioner gains a cohesive personality because his decision was so monumental and total, so unconditional and absolute. When it comes to Existence's Truth and its Path to Pure Mind, there are no conditions attached with surrender; therefore, you must first fully understand the practice methods, knowing that you cannot ask for special conditions or bargain for change when embarking on the Circle of Life's living course. Our definition of surrender should be interpreted as a letting go of the self; for example, there can be no "if you do, then I'll comply." Etc.

Having let go, a student projects this attitude at all times. It becomes obvious to all what his life practice represents. With surrender, a student becomes totally receptive to Existence's Breath of Life and is in communion with the Nature of Existence.

INTROSPECTION
Awaken Through Meditation

The Meditative State is a transcendence of the normal worldly conscious mind to be conscious through one of the many spiritual dimensions.

Practitioners on the Path to Pure Mind depend solely on the effectiveness of the Pure Mind practice, not on erroneous beliefs. As it is with other practices, its guidelines do not include impressing upon a student's mind a belief system in place of self-awakening.

A practitioner on the Path to Pure Mind will never hear his guide say, "I believe this to be true." He will hear only the how-to of reaching beyond to the spiritual dimensions. These two ways of expressing knowledge and methodology are worlds apart.

There are three primaries plus many other secondary considerations for Pure Mind meditation practice, and each one calls for a different technique, but all play an essential role in man's becoming awakened. The first is to satisfy set requirements in order to create a vessel of purified energies. Second is our creation of the binders that harness this energy vessel. The third is to perfect control and movement of this vessel.

What then is meditation? Putting it simply, it is the door we must go through in order to open our capacities. Meditation is, in fact, a natural part of our nature, and when we relax ourselves into ourselves, into the very moment, we open and expand our natural capacity for learning, for creativity, for love, and compassion. After a while, we come to understand it is our only way to true freedom.

Meditation is being in a high state of consciousness and should not be confused with the techniques and methods which are just tools to help transport man to the meditative state.

The reasons we meditate on the Path to Pure Mind are: *We meditate in order to attain extraction of self, thereby affecting the freedom of our mind/body. This is accomplished, in part, by mindfulness, which is one way of bringing all the contents of conscious experience into harmony with a common center.*

We meditate to be in union with the silence that resides in all form and existed before all form, before all thought, and before any gods.

We meditate to understand awakenings, animals, plants, and all of nature that has been trying hard to educate us throughout our sentient lives.

We meditate to know our emotions, to understand the emptiness of our ego, so that we may clearly watch the thoughts that arise and fade away.

We meditate because we are at home in pure absolute silence even though we are surrounded by sounds of talking, machines, our own bodies, and our ever-busy minds.

We meditate to give up attachments, like pain for when we let go, we give ourselves up and dissolve into silence.

FREEDOM, the ultimate state: Freedom allows humans just to be their higher selves, free from tension and stress, free from worry and suffering, free from the oppressions of the past, free just to be and live fully in the moment of now, and free from the burdens of sickness and death. In order to know how to gain back the seemingly lost freedom, one must first identify the culprit that robs them of that which they prize so highly, the moments of their lives.

Man tends to look outside himself for this culprit and blames whatever is taking place at the moment, whether it be their job, marriage, children, parents, peers, government, actually any distraction can be a culprit. Man's outward search goes on ceaselessly, but the real culprit, the one that truly robs us of our life is our own out of control mind, and it resides inside.

Previously I stated that meditation is the door we must go through so that we may open our full potential, but what is the key that opens that door? It is us, in a state as a spectator. This spectator is a detached itness to our body and mind functions as well as to our relationship to all things. This spectator is our spiritual side which knows who, what, and why we are. This knowledge when awakened allows us to accept our ourselves as we truly are, and that knowledge is the only true freedom. This freedom from mind allows all other spiritual freedoms into our lives. Meditation shows us how to discover the spectator within ourselves. The door and the key are, of course, metaphors and they should not be considered as separate because they work simultaneously.

We may see meditation as a farmer might see the earth; he must first cultivate the earth's soil to prepare it for planting and the growing of crops, whereas we must first construct a perfect frame of mental awareness so that we are instantly ready to absorb what is revealed to us from Existence's nature.

There are numerous veils that obscure man's Existence's Nature. The most prominent are: form, ego, will, consciousness, emotions, fear, and dualistic thinking. These veils can only be lifted when seen as non-reality. Man's hungry ghost will be quenched when he knows himself not as separate but as one with Existence's Nature and all its physical forms.

In a high state of consciousness, man comes to know how wondrous he can be and fully realize that only in his mind/body does he have the ability to become a perpetual spiritual and physical energy that gives life and light to all.

Man is fully expressed when he advances inward to an awakening of completeness, and he actualizes that in the way he thinks and lives.

The catch is, in order to reach that awakening of completeness man must first live and think that way, he must either start with or eventually come to the Path of Pure Mind meditation.

The Mind: the mind plays an important part in meditation. Foremost is the creation of pure energy, visualization through imagination, contemplation, interpreting the awakening experience, and the seeking of Existence's Breath of Knowledge which is the transmitter of Truth. Done correctly some meditations have a way of breaking the walls in the mind helping to fulfill man's purpose.

The contemplative state is frustrating to man because it can be seen as a passive state, but at the same time, it is an intensely active process. It is a state without an object center; therefore, we have nothing to concentrate on, yet it has all the intensity of deep concentration.

Contemplation has no thought process, yet it is called by man meditation. In a state of contemplation, man can achieve awareness without attachment. It is knowing without a subject who knows or an object that is known. Although this state is very remote and inaccessible to most, the constant and devoted practice of the Path to Pure Mind will allow the state to reveal itself.

There are as many varied tools as there are Paths that have been forged over the centuries to help us reach a meditative state. For example, there is counting the breath, watching the breath, feeling the breath, watching the rising and lowering of the diaphragm as we breathe, controlling the breath, not controlling the breath, on and on. Then too, there are all those other techniques like dancing, humming, sexual contact, and whirling. What must be understood is that **there are different means used for whatever you are trying to accomplish with meditation.** On the Path to Pure Mind, we must achieve many different things, and we reside in many different states, in and out of physical forms. So, you can understand the tools of meditation change with the aim. The correct methods used for the Path to Pure Mind will follow.

Attaining nonattachment of thoughts and emotions while in a meditative state, most of which arise from the constant input of data from the senses, must be let go and that is crucial.

Deep Third Eye Meditation: there are three very important factors in the Path to Pure Mind third eye meditation. Success depends on man recognizing his third eye, recognizing the role of himself as a spectator, and him having acute awareness or attentiveness. This deep meditation is both highly dynamic and commonly passive at the same time. When successful it allows pure energies to be created while a quieting of the mind takes place which creates the opportunity for awakening experiences to arise. With this technique there lies the key to unlocking the spiritual dimensions the practitioner seeks.

Normally in a nonfunctioning state, the third eye awaits man's evolutionary process to go beyond his "now" self and become active. The third eye can be opened by simple methods, but it takes knowledge of its existence, patience, and a lot of practice to do so. With the correct method and attraction, a magnetic drawing from man's third eye starts to take you in. It is from inside the third eye that man begins to see the outside relative world in a single, non-dualistic mode of awareness. Man sees as a spectator.

Starting with such attentiveness, the third eye leads man to the freedom of seeing things in terms of their fitness for knowledge instead of as a composition of aggregates, and having attained a clear, quiet mind man develops a state of acute awareness. This state evokes the Existence's Breath of Knowledge. And that state allows man to experience the awakening process.

Old mystical Scriptures speak of deep attentive awareness as the means of opening the third eye. A concentrated effort can bring about the experience of seeing your thoughts racing in front of you and not inside your head. It is at that point that you are the spectator, not the player of mental pinball.

In man's life they are what they think, they are the players and therefore the game itself, but in the phenomenal state where they are the observers, the witnesses, the spectators, they can observe their pains, their physical and mental suffering, understand from whence they came, and how, in fact, they have no identity, no life, unless we give it to them by identifying with and attaching them to ourselves.

The paradoxical question of if you become a spectator who is watching you or if you are the spectator? The simple answer is the third eye is the spectator, and you, by seeing solely through this third eye become as one the spectator itself. This happening, as always, must be experienced. It cannot be judged by outsiders or understood with words.

By opening the third eye we see beyond our breathing and our breath, and we can actually know the breath's essence, or the breath within the breath, which is Existence's Breath of Knowledge. Reaching this state, we can feel its energy, see its form, know its nature, and experience a true living joy. *It is here that you stand poised and awakenings come. It happens. We know, and so can you!*

When you add the joy to the love contained in awakening, it's like building a new life-based on Truth of purpose, a perfect design, and strong binding energies.

Energy Movement and Imagination: the most important thing to know of energy movement is that willpower, desire, needs, and the like will not move energy.

We must first learn to move our energies by imagination. We have been led to believe that imagination is this a cerebral activity and therefore useless in everyday life realities, when in fact imagination is much more when related to spirituality.

Imagination: is an actual vehicle that helps carry Pure Mind practitioners to unknown spiritual realms and dimensions. Thought and feeling energies aid in strengthening our imagination.

What is imagination? On the one hand, our power to imagine seems to be illogical and irrational, yet it is our imagination that helps us realize our greatest goals. Great accomplishments of technology, music, art, and discovery begin with creative images that were conceived in the realm of imagination. We remain skeptical because we are taught that the imagination creates solutions, but we admire its unending creativity. We are extremely uncomfortable with our fear of not being able to control it, yet we are fascinated by the possibilities it offers us. We doubt its use in the face of logic, but we wish we had more of it. We feel that somehow imagination goes the way of childhood, lost forever, but in fact, it's just buried beneath layers of social conditioning. Practicality, not imagination, is supposed to enable an economically stressed society to function. For most of man this may be true, but to move society forward, we must use our imagination.

For the student of Pure Mind meditation, imagination means more than dreaming (mental masturbation, if you will): *it is a vital and primary vehicle because it helps connect us with Existence's Breath of Knowledge. It also helps connect us with energies in all things.*

Imagination skills require breaking the walls man creates in his attempt to master the physical and cultural ways of modern life. The breaking of those walls must be accomplished so that man may reestablish the bond between the physical and the spiritual worlds.

The means we have of creating a line of communication with the world of energy is critical in creating and later maintaining an eternal state. This eternal state is the vehicle made up of man's created pure energies, combined with the energies he has attracted then further bound together with the embodiment of love, kindness, and sprinkled with his untainted personality traits.

The method used in the Path to Pure Mind is totally interactive with the environment, Existence's Breath of Knowledge, and Nature. It is, therefore, very powerful and creates a lot of movement. What man is doing is mobilizing his energy's forces and through the power of his mind and emotions sending them out to intercede and communicate with all other energies that exist both in this world and beyond. Man must understand that he doesn't always control the events that he experiences, but he does control his responses. The more active his imagination, the more powerful he is and the greater the volume of energies attracted for his energy vehicle. To be successful is to break down the walls between the world of ordinary reality and the spiritual dimensions.

Imagineering can be slowly relearned by walled-in humans. One small step at a time, successfully completed, and you may find yourself sitting on a cloud enjoying the view of this Earth.

Awakening one's senses: all our senses must be used for creating images and infusing them with life. Since our goal is to have our imaginary creation, experiences, and forms transformed into reality, we must fully develop all of our senses to their optimum.

Seekers must utilize simple exercises to accomplish honing our senses to the fullest. This is very important because your senses stimulate your imagination back into detailed use and enable you to create, re-create, and empower these creations with energy and therefore life. It is a beginning for the human to fulfill his purpose in nature.

On my cushion sitting quietly
all my restlessness stills,
like circles on water, it will fade away.
My burdens lie where they lie,
where I left them,

adrift in their own way.
Fear rises. I enter into my fear,
become my fear, then what I fear
from my fear leaves me,
soon it's my fear that evaporates.
With my fears dying moan
my ego lets go and
my heart joyfully opens.

THE PURE MIND PATH
A Living Practice

The embodiment of Universal Nature's moral code, fulfillment of man's need to awaken, to define, to adjust evolutionary Paths, and to energize latent possibilities are the aims of Pure Mind practice and are, in part, the practice itself.

Whether one is awakening or reawakening is of no consequence; the practice remains the same. The Pure Mind Practice to reincarnation is the only true Path fulfilling humanity's life purpose. It does this by taking us beyond the limited expectation of our human body/mind nature to a spiritual dimension where we gather and bind pure, undefiled energies and secure an energy vessel. This is the highest possible aim of any human. Therefore the practice should be taken up in a mental attitude befitting such a great purpose.

Keeping in mind the true significance of a reincarnated being, that a creator of future phenomena working hand-in-hand with Universal Nature instills confidence in the student. This confidence begins with awakening to the heart of Universal Nature, which is also important for the meditative process. Once a student totally surrenders to the Pure Mind practice, he relaxes into a meditative and acutely aware life. Having learned the definitive purpose of life, he acquires a great deal of conviction, which fills him with further confidence and joy. Awakening to his capacity inspires a determined attitude to attain the deepest enlightenment and reach the highest spiritual state. Surrender, recognition, and relaxation are the prime movers. Surrendering the ego in favor of a blissful union with Universal Nature unlocks the natural energy channels and Truth flows unhindered.

In one way the Pure Mind Practice is very strict, because the time to practice is the entire day and every day, and the place of practice is anywhere and everywhere. We are speaking of our embodying and manifesting Universal Nature's morality and codes. Together with a high state of mindfulness is how a student conducts his activities throughout his life.

One of the most important activities of the practice is meditation. There are two different aims for meditation on the Path. Therefore, there are different methods. First, there are the awakening meditation methods. Secondly, there are the energy building and gathering methods. In the case of beginning students, I found that silent sitting meditation is the best to start. Until a student seeker conquers all restlessness and pain becoming totally relaxed within the sitting position, he should not attempt to go beyond. The silent sitting position he adopts will be the basic position for most of the advanced methods, so he must be totally at ease and able to sustain it for extended periods of time. For more information and procedures in silent sitting practice (Zazen) choose any Zen Buddhist instruction book and follow its methods. Bringing yourself to a point where you are able to advance may take anywhere from one to three years, dependent on your physical and mental conditioning when you begin, and how you progress.

In this practice we do nothing to stand out, nothing to set us apart. Most religions and spiritual practices that bestow titles, robes of position, and various other artifacts should be scrutinized for the egotistical and/or control factors that are supported by this type of habitual nonsense. This is especially true of the practices that teach unity of all things, but nevertheless, impose separation and status hierarchies. Teachers should be judged by their actions, deeds, and presence, not by their rank, or what they wear, or write, or say.

Students of the Pure Mind Path reach a point in their practice where they realize their ignorance in attaining the physical and mental balances that must be achieved for them to rise above their present spiritual state. Turning their thinking to the basic Truth of an existing natural order, they can separate their conditioned behavior patterns from what the human's nature and the Universal Natures intended. Eating and drinking in accordance with strict healthy dietary laws place man's systems in balance, and further, leads him to the state allowing unification, creative contemplation, and the realm of high spirituality.

Diseases are created by the ingestion of toxic food, water, and air they influence the mind which gathered impurity from our physical body's diseased condition, our imagined fears, our acceptance of perverted truth, as well as our environment. The human mind creates stress, frustration, and emotional disappointments through many forms of wrong understanding. This is particularly true in our adaptation of diluted partial truth belief systems both in the social and spiritual realms. If we are to have spiritual development, we must eliminate all these layers of impurities.

The Pure Mind Path, which is a mirror reflection of Universal Nature itself, has been split into many disciplines dating as far back as existence itself. One example of this splintering is the old Yogic sciences which itself has split into two branches, the healing and the spiritual, and now has been split even further beyond its physical and mental practices and study. Even so, separate or together, any successful effort by a student of any discipline largely depends upon a mind/body that is free from disease.

All Yogic and Buddhist practices stem from Pure Mind awakenings and methods. Though greatly diluted they nevertheless contain many seeds of Truth and methodology inherited from their mother discipline. The one overpowering and gravely solemn truth that has been totally distorted, vilified or forgotten is that; *The fulfillment of our true nature is a matter of becoming, not just a matter of being. That is the ultimate wisdom beyond wisdom.*

Think! Do not allow yourselves to continue to be educated and conditioned so to be exploited by the system. If you do not break your chains, you will never know the freedom, love, and joys that highly spiritual achievers experience.

Seekers on the Path toward the awakening of Universal Truth are greatly dictated by the condition of the vehicle in which they travel, how they use that vehicle, and the tracks they travel on. Everything about us is made up of energy. The foods we eat, the air we breathe, the liquids we drink, the chemicals we ingest, the thoughts we think, and the emotions we feel form our vehicle. Each time we eat a nutritionless, processed, or chemically laden food, sip polluted water, inhale polluted air, cause abuse and killing of a sentient being we, taint our bodies and minds with disease and in turn, we taint our energy. Tainted energy will be created by a disease and/or unbalanced mind and body. Unless we make every effort to rid ourselves of unnatural substances, we will fail in our life's purpose as humans.

Meditation, chanting, work, relationships, dancing, walking, exercising, etc. are some of the uses of our vehicle. Meditative practice, the books we read, the teacher, and our destination are the tracks we travel on. It is wrong to think that these separate parts make up the whole of one's being. The important principle of binding, or polarization, is missing. Whether in the phenomenon world, spiritual dimensions or the internal vessel we create, all are bound by Universal Nature via its awakenings. The old quote, "There is nothing new under the sun," can be seen as coming from the realization that all things reflect all things. The eternal principle of being In-Perpetuum reflects Universal Nature, as an In-Perpetuum being's eternal energy vessel reflects Universal Nature's infinite existence.

Students of the Pure Mind Path constantly live their whole life as a reflection of Universal Nature which binds all natures, and that is our practice.

THE HEART AND SOUL
of the Pure Mind Practice

Love, Kindness, Compassion, and Sensitivity

**"If Truth is indeed in and around everything
How is it that I cannot see it?"
"Simply because you are in the way."**

Love: Love is, in fact, a mind state that is contrary to any hope of lasting happiness. This love is the mind's delusionary state which it settles for the futile search for fullness.

Since we have been trained to use our minds to solve problems, to create or gather whatever we need from sources outside ourselves, we naturally look for that which is beyond; beyond our belief systems, beyond our reason, etc. Because we have turned to books, teachers, and profits in the search for fullness, or "love," we have unwittingly turned our attention outward, and so depend on others to define who we are. We choose marriage or life partners who are willing to give us what we seek and to further inflate our egos by providing approval and acceptance. These people we label compatible, and there are millions upon millions of loving couples born out of these false impressions which are pathological in nature. This mental or physical "love" is illusory, because it drains energy and brings nothing more than short-term physical or ego satisfaction and leaves us in a long-term state of frustration and boredom.

Not knowing nor finding anything more fulfilling humans try unsuccessfully to substitute this illusionary love for something most people unknowingly but deeply long for eternal life with its joyful state of ecstasy. This longing or hungry ghost is a natural drive from Universal Nature to fulfill itself through all physical phenomena. There is no way of escaping this desire and no way to fulfill it from the outside.

It is fruitless to seek as "love" the illusions which are born out of the mind for fulfillment of sexual drives and various emotions that stem from the same desirous nature. Seek and find true love which is born inside through a pure meditative state that attracts awakenings. This is love, which has no expectations, is conceived with Universal Nature, is carried and spread by awakenings from Universal Truth. It is only this love that delivers fullness and eternal joy.

Deep awakenings bring an all-encompassing love that arises with the quality of understanding that spreads through and out of our body and mind. Here the enlightened find fullness because they are totally consumed and thereby become love itself. When in a true meditative state everything starts to disappear, thought, physical pain, stress, everything, until there's nothing left except silence. It is not the rational understanding of a silent noiseless void, instead, the living silence that overflows with deep rich sound tones and a light that can only be seen by "seeing eyes" turned inward.

This love found in meditation and awakening is not directed towards anybody; it is not a relationship but a quality of our being. We are not "in love," we are unconditional love, and loving unconditionally is eternal.

Kindness: Is the embodiment of the deep love experienced living the teachings of Pure Mind with its meditation direction. It is the practice of kindness shown directly to all living things.

That is, treating every living thing in a kind and gentle manner. The principle is to cause no physical or mental harm or abuse, neither directly nor indirectly through our desires.

An act of kindness, without an ulterior motive is a pure way of giving up man's idea of separateness and is an awakening of "oneness." "All of a single root." In acts of kindness man should proclaim no distinction between man and woman, teacher and student, earth and sky, and know that everything has the same value, everything is just as it is.

All spiritual teachings and awakenings will be in vain if we do not manifest the love we garner into kindness and compassion. Contrary to some popular religious separatist beliefs, even the most exalted states and spiritual accomplishments become useless unless one lives his life with kindness. Knowing that love, kindness, and compassion play a major part in creating the binding energies of our energy vessel proves beyond a doubt that living in kindness is extremely necessary and valuable.

Compassion: compassion is something which is inherent in the human being. It is not merely an applied something because of its creation. In the Pure Mind Path, man will awaken and become the actualization of compassion. He learns to know the pain of suffering by others, but more importantly he learns to understand its roots, and finally how-to bring suffering to an end. All these combined lead man to know that with his awakening and the love it brings all things will benefit. Compassion is not the goal for it is not a goal of Universal Nature, but instead a natural result of one's successful efforts. When compassion is awakened, compassion will be manifested.

What you own and how you think is how you will be remembered. But is that what you truly are?

Compassion is one of a student's strongest awakenings. It will gently touch and caress you. This releases a feeling of ecstasy which fills you with joy, and the energy created explodes and pulsates and can be felt by others. Some call it your vibrations, and by those, you will be fondly remembered.

Sensitivity: walking the Pure Mind Path, a seeker learns that the world and everything in it does not belong to him nor should they be possessed by him. It is not his to use and abuse for his comfort and pleasure. Instead, on the Path one learns that they belong to everything in this world, and in the universe. Earthly humans are a miniscule part of it; they are not the heart of it. The Earth does not, nor should it be made to revolve around him. When man awakens to these Truths, he becomes sensitive to even the smallest of creatures, and they become important to him. Man must understand that even an amoeba is as important as the sun for without its existence he would be less. This amoeba is not replaceable; it has its own value, its own evolution.

Sensitivity creates a closeness with nature, with its animals, its flowers, its forests, its mountains, lakes, and rivers. It brings you so much closer to the stars, moons, and other universes with their living beings. As sensitivity grows so grows love, and as love grows as a student your energy vessel becomes more and more solidified, and you get closer to becoming an eternal being.

To live and love fully requires us to recognize and accept that we cannot possess nor own anything. This applies to material things as well as other people and includes our own bodies. Students know that spiritual joy, freedom, and wisdom do not come as a result of possession, but rather through their capacity to open themselves enabling them to love more fully. The longing for and the movement towards love are some other forms of the hungry spiritual ghost that resides in all of humanity and is behind most of our activities.

Most happiness that we experience in our lives is never about possessions or understanding, but about our ability to love, to be free, and to have a wise relationship with our own lives. This awakening arises out of a sense of connection with all things.

Living a spiritual life may seem to most as complicated, but in actuality, it is the opposite. We find that simplicity leads to clarity even in the midst of this complex world. We can discover these things when we realize that it's the quality of the love, compassion, and kindness that we bring to our lives that matters the most.

Without the Pure Mind Path body of knowledge, and understanding, the essence of love, kindness, and compassion, meditation exercises that point you to awakening are a waste of effort.

Awakening is not the focus of the Pure Mind practice. To guide practitioners to open themselves like the petals of a rose is its object and therefore the focal point.

<u>Mindfulness</u>
**"Truth lies in the grass and in the soil.
Those who see take off their shoes." -E. B. Browning**

**"Try and be a sheet of paper with nothing on it.
Be a spot of ground where nothing is growing,
where something might be planted,
a seed, possibly from the Absolute." - Rumi**

Mindfulness: Mindfulness in everyday life and in meditation is in itself a practice of the highest priority. Without it, there can be no meditative state or would meaningful life be possible. Mindfulness is a state of being in this very moment, at this very moment.

Man must live solely in each present moment with an attitude of a spectator, that is, the "self" that sees with pure observation, and it is through this attitude that clear knowledge can be obtained. The practice of mindfulness brings man's mind under control and to a state of rest helping to bring insight into the threefold itness of I, us, and universality, (seeing something as it is, as a separate form with its own nature and at the same time as one with its immediate surrounding and further with the universe) *and thus to a clear insight of the Universal Nature of all existence. Seen in this way mindfulness can be a basis for deep awakening.*

Throughout Pure Mind meditation practice, we create a state of clear awareness, or mindfulness, and give to each experience our full attention. This is how we recognize when any part of our lives and/or meditation practice is deteriorating so we may correct it at that very moment. A Pure Mind life must be lived with a mindful attitude because this makes you aware of your activities in every moment. It is through Pure Mind practice that you will find the meaning of life as a sentient being, and then you will have the meaning of your everyday activity. Living this way, we are not special; we are, in fact, just living in the manner everyone should.

Right mindfulness is the blood that flows through seekers of Truth and the core of a seekers practice. Being mindful is the key to knowing the mind and thus the starting point. This is the perfect tool for shaping the mind and thus the focal point of Pure Mind practice.

Since the state of In-Perpetuum life is the ultimate manifestation of Pure Mind practice, and that practice depends greatly upon right mindfulness, becoming an In-Perpetuum Being can also be said to be the culminating point.

Mindfulness is also the prime function of consciousness; without it, we have no perception of any object at all. When an object stimulates the senses, attention is aroused in its basic form, and an initial first notice takes place. This happens thousands of times during every second of our waking lives. This initial attention is of decisive importance for it is the first "touching" of the subconscious by the conscious.

In this first perception phase only a very general and indistinct picture of the object results. If there is any further interest in the object or if its impact on our senses is very strong, our attention will be focused on the details. Now our attention will be directed towards its characteristics, also on its direct relationship to us. Here is where our mind compares its present perception with similar ones recollected from our past. This is exactly how we coordinate our experiences. This stage is a crucial step in mental development and shows the close and constant connection between memory and mindfulness, or attention. Without memory, attention towards an object would give us merely isolated facts, as in the case of most of the perceptions of animals. This is important and should be understood. **It is from this associative thinking that the next crucial step in evolutionary development is derived.** Here we must include the capacity of abstract thinking in this second stage of cognition being affected by the development of mindfulness. So, we can see four characteristics of this second stage: an increase in detail; reference to the observer, or subjectivity; connective or associative thinking; and abstract thinking.

The second stage of cognition perception is certainly more detailed and comprehensive, but it is not necessarily more reliable. Perception is more or less adulterated by contaminated memory. For instance, association, emotions, intellectual prejudices, wishful thinking, etc., and primarily by the delusion of either a conscious or an unconscious assumption of a permanent substance inherent in things or of a soul in living things, will cause this unreliable perception.

Because of any or all of these factors, the reliability of even the most common perceptions and judgments may be seriously impaired. Without guidance an overwhelming percentage of people remain stuck in the second stage of perception; these include those who do not apply this knowledge to the systematic training of their minds.

Gradually advancing in the development of attentiveness, students enter the domain of right mindfulness. It is called right because it keeps the mind free from false influences because it is the basis of right understanding because it teaches student/seekers to do the right things in the right way.

The objects of perception and thought, having gone through the sifting process of keen analysis as prepared by right mindfulness, are therefore reliable material for all other advanced mental functions such as theory evolution and judgment, ethical decisions, etc., and most notably these now undistorted actualities form a solid basis for Pure Mind meditation; for example, viewing all phenomena as impermanent and void of substance. Undistorted actualities also form the basis of the Pure Mind everyday living practice. The elevated level of clarity offered by right mindfulness will, to an unprepared mind be anything but familiar.

At best an untrained mind may occasionally touch the edge of undistorted clarity, but in treading the way dictated by Pure Mind right mindfulness it can grow into something very familiar. Right mindfulness performs the same functions as the two lowest stages of development though it does this on a much higher plane.

The functions common to right mindfulness produce an increasingly greater clarity and intensity of consciousness, presenting an image of actuality that increasingly filters out any falsifications.

With this brief outline of the evolution of mental processes as mirrored by the actual stages and quality differences of perception, we can see the faint awareness of the object becoming a more distinct perception and gain a more detailed knowledge of it. Traveling from the perception of isolated facts to the discovery of their casual mental connections, we go from a still defective, inaccurate, or prejudiced cognition to the clear and undistorted presentation by right mindfulness. We have also seen how it is an increase in intensity and quality of attentive mindfulness that is mainly instrumental in the transition to the next highest dimension.

The mind functions to attach objects to memory. In doing so, it expands. What is mind if not an accumulation of memories of thoughts, objects, and experiences? As we gather these things, our minds expand. One of the great awakenings has shown that every day more and more junk is collected. Your mind grows bigger and bigger, but you have less and less consciousness. Man is consistently repeating thoughts, and these thoughts are a repetition of our accumulated past.

Thinking is never original because man can only think in terms of the known. Nothing new comes through. You cannot think about the unknown; you can only reach the unknown when you are not thinking.

Let the past rest in the past; think only this moment. The irony of this is that if you are really in this moment, you cannot think; it is not possible.

Remain in the moment. Live moment to moment; forget your past as well as the future, so that whatever you are doing becomes meditative.

For example, when you look at a weed and really see it, the weed is no longer just a weed, and you are no longer just you. The weed and you dissolve into something beyond what can be explained logically, but we experience it. This is clear seeing without thought, and we may understand the pure elation of as-it-is-ness, suchness, or itness.

So, we have two different usages of the word mindfulness. In its simplest form, we see it as "being there," that is being in the very moment, and we have the more complex of usage, as in right perception of reality; but both definitions are codependent and therefore each cannot exist without the other.

An example of "being there":
just sitting
my mind empty,
so, I threw it away

An example of a right perception of reality:
without me
he wouldn't exist
no Temple Gardens

PURE MIND UNDERSTANDING
Ultimate Truth Transcends Logical Thought

Analytical, logical, linear, systematic, and scientific thought processes employed by scholars, scientists, intellectuals, and the like are a totally useless means of reaching an understanding of Universal Truths that lie beyond the physical dimensions. Using these methods of thinking when attempting to understand spiritual dimensions and realities therein always come up empty and frustrating. And yet they will dismiss, out of hand, what their minds cannot grasp.

The following is not a metaphor, nor an analogy, nor is it based on intuition, nor simply one possibility among many. It is Universal Truth, and it should be taken literally. Until the "mind types" reach beyond their mind's physical limitations to spiritual realities, they will probably view this as fantasy. So be it!

<u>Reincarnation:</u> it is the process of increasing one's existence infinitely. There is only one Way to achieve the state of eternal being with perpetual life cycles, and that is with Pure Mind awakening and embodiment.

Those who see promises or threats in that statement are unsuitable for Pure Mind practice. There are no threats or promises with this Truth; only in man's interpretation of it.

Hearing the teachings and creation of an energy vessel with the karmic effect of an In-Perpetuum Being requires many things from an individual: a deep practice, the creation and sustaining of purifying energies from his body/mind, awakening at all levels, and the embodiment of those awakenings. The pure energies a student creates attaches to the created vessel enabling those energies to dissolve continually back into themselves. The binding energies which hold the vessel together are created by the awakenings and manifestation of purified energy and unconditional love.

The sum of all a student's purified energies including enlightened thoughts, correct attitudes, personality traits, etc., dissolve into the initial created purified vessel of energy. This newly expanded vessel dissolves into itself, and that self dissolves into itself. This process continues until the student transcends to the point where he is wholly an energy vessel. This vessel spontaneously evolves to the state of a perpetual energy being that is totally liberated from mind and body forms.

Having reached the state of an In-Perpetuum Being, this vessel remains in the formless state of timelessness and spacelessness until it returns as a sentient human form. This first reincarnation is without personal choice of form, time, or galaxy unless the form was defined by a reincarnate while the student was still in the physical form of his awakening. From then on, while in the physical state of reincarnation, he can choose his own identity, either as a sentient or not. If he chooses not, he may choose a still further reincarnation to return as a sentient. It is their choice is just to return as part of the evolution without defining, as was the case for his original reincarnation.

Through the practice of the Pure Mind Path students of awakening learn to recognize that all the virtuous aspects which made up their personalities and permeated their actions by living the Pure Mind way persist after shedding body/mind. This is due to the pure energy vessel and the binding energies they created. They also fully understand that all things are impermanent because as they go from chosen form to chosen form and from aeon to aeon, their energy vessel changes. Just as some adhere to this practice and gradually evolve from sentient beings to Beings In-Perpetuum, so will they evolve from that perpetual being to their new life form, bringing with them their relatively long-term characteristics which help determine their "now" personalities.

This knowledge that character and personality preexist in reincarnation (impermanency is a matter of form, partial form, degree, and time) makes it easy to understand the recognition of heredity factors seen in reincarnates.

Freeing the mind/body
my mortality
became immortal.
-sastitz

Creation: "In the beginning, God created heaven and earth." This is the start of the Old Testament. Let me ask you, was this God a spirit, a person, a thing? Was it male, female, or both? Did it have a consciousness and why did he, she, or it, create?

The Bible's proclamation of God's creation and all the questions that statement raises can lead your mind far away into an imaginary beyond, and when you imagine an omnipotent "God" as a premise, all the conclusions that you arrive at will only be yours or others imagination at work. What if the creator of which the Bible speaks was actually "thought"? Such thought that leads straight back to mind and heart. You may begin to recognize how instead of leading you to an imaginary beyond, the recognition of thought as the basis for creation leads to a solid starting point: the mind. This mind becomes the focal point, and when it is liberated and purified, the mind becomes the culminating point.

Through mind alone, man will be aware of the external world including his body, so it follows that if he can understand this "mind," he will have placed himself in a position to understand all things. To do this man must turn inward to find the Path leading beyond the boundaries of his own ego mind. This can be a very slow process, but if the methods are practiced correctly, with loving kindness and compassion, the answers never fail to arrive. Man will find that there is a strong and well-ordered inner center deep in his mind, where all this confusion can dissolve, and energy forces can spontaneously gather around Universal Nature revealing to him its knowledge in a perfect way.

Man must recognize that the center of his mind which is so much a part of him is unknown to him; that the conscious mind which he sees as unwieldy and obstinate can with significant effort be made pliant; that the "freeing" of the mind is something he can accomplish in his lifetime.

In the beginning of any universal cycle which at that exact moment is the end of the previous cycle, there is Existence and its Universal Nature. Therein resides a realm of all latent possibilities, and wherein resides Universal Nature's single, powerful, and perpetual thought: to know itself. To know its Self Nature beyond self, including the nature, manifestation, and final evolution stage of all mental and physical possibilities. Because of this pure, powerful thought, a single latent possibility is energized by the one remaining In-Perpetuum energy vessel whose sole objective is to do just that: energize the one possibility which starts the cycle of a new universe.

Through countless light years of Existence's need to know, "In-Perpetuum Beings" energize most of the remaining latent possibilities. When all phenomena evolve nearing their natural end, all sentient beings will have reached their highest state of consciousness. They, in turn, direct their thoughts to a single thought of knowing, the knowing of that which is yet to be known. At the same time, all remaining latent phenomena are energized and manifested, and they come to be fully known. Beyond this point, all evolutionary life processes come to their natural end. With this "end" there is a "beginning" for as always, all that remains is: existence and Universal Nature with its one powerful thought to know itself, and therein lies its realm of latent possibilities, and therein resides a single In-Perpetuum Being again with its one powerful objective....

> We shall not cease from exploration,
> and that the end of all our exploring
> we will arrive where we started
> and know the place for the very first time. - T.S. Elliot

Man's means of exploration beyond the physical realms is the Path to Pure Mind with its awakened Truths because of its practice places mind/body in the right motion. This direction polarizes and expands the energy vessel which when liberated from the physical remains as an In-Perpetuum Being. This being's ultimate purpose is to be an Energizer of all the phenomena possibilities.

"It is best not to seek that which is seemingly far away, beyond the realm of experience and therefore beyond our comprehension when you cannot even see what is very close to you." - Unknown

Origin is no less or more than a combining of energy with a latent possibility having its own nature. It is from these origins that all phenomena flow. Phenomena differ from universal cycle to cycle, because each time a possibility is energized to life, it bears the "personality signature" of the energy essence consciousness from which it sprang, and yet it is basically always the same, for all phenomena is inundated with Universal Nature.

Student practitioners of the Path to Pure Mind will come to unravel life's mysteries as they travel beyond their limited minds to a union with Universal Nature and become acquainted with their own origin. They are travelers who pass on in haste and separate from self as smoke separates from the fire. Their travels are a succession of Truths awakened, leading them away from darkness and dualistic thinking.

They travel upward, higher and higher, transfiguring their vessel with more and more energy and binding it more solidly with uncompromised love until they separate from body/mind to become or remain as In-Perpetuum Beings.

The illusionary world of what lies beyond in the spiritual realms, as with the basis of most religions, rests on incorrect interpretations of partial realities. A person's illusions are very real to him, and they create a great deal of tainted energy, an energy usually enhanced by false joy and momentary happiness. In the near future, the loss of the same joy and happiness will bring him a great amount of suffering, emptiness, and disillusionment.

With a tainted spiritual search, imagination leads a person to the point, as in formal religions, where one's practice becomes only a belief system and only blind acceptance remains as an answer. You may come to a point where the practice takes you as far as it is able, as with Zen Buddhism, a practice that may take you beyond the human condition of suffering as was described by the historical Buddha, and is, as I see it, the basis for modern psychology. However, if the Zen boat or any other vehicle has taken you to its limits, it's time to bow out and find "the" boat that will carry you to the point of total awakening and imminent immortality. The path to Pure Mind does exactly that by progressing beyond the point where all others stop; beyond faith, to the experience of the deepest awakenings.

When first energized by an In-Perpetuum Being, a species has the purity of that which has not yet been contaminated by the human mind. Contamination begins as a species materializes into form and the start of its evolution. The moment before materialization is when unenlightened beings see this event as a "miracle," as a God like revelation because knowledge of its true origin is beyond man's level of human consciousness.

Ultimately all origination is no more or less than a combining of energy with a latent possibility having its own nature. It is from this event that all phenomena flow. Energizing can only take place after an In-Perpetuum Being passes out of physical form. Yet all definitions of possibility take place while they're in physical human form.

<u>Suffering:</u> Buddhism did not begin with the answers to great metaphysical questions like, "What is the meaning of life? What happens when we die?" And/or proving the existence of God. Rather its root principle is that all human existence is imperfect in a very deep way. Therefore, "Suffering I teach, and the way out of suffering," the Buddha declared and began teaching the doctrine of the Four Noble Truths. His first truth: Suffering exists. His second truth: Suffering has an identifiable course. Third truth: The causes of suffering can be terminated. Fourth truth: It is the means of its elimination.

These Four Noble Truths have been interpreted, commented on, and reinterpreted. All of these being housed in great bodies of work and commentaries on those works. Unfortunately, like the words of Jesus Christ and many others, most of the essence and therefore the true meaning of what was and is being transmitted was misinterpreted.

All of humanity's existence is characterized by suffering which cannot bring satisfaction in any healthy form. Due to man's level of understanding and life practice, people experience suffering in everything they do; birth, sickness, death, having the experiences they do not like, being separated from that which they do like, and not obtaining what they desire. Add the principle traits of attachment: form, sensations, perception, mental formations, and consciousness. Since craving and desire attach themselves to those traits, it makes them objects of attachments which will cause suffering and all its illusions. Further, still sensual cravings and ego desires bind humans to illusion.

Truth and the standard interpretations are widely separated. The true meaning and essence of dispelling suffering are that all sentient human beings exist for the purpose of liberating their body and minds from suffering and in the process will aid in liberating themselves from suffering and further invoke the true karmic law of eternal being.

Cause and effect (karma): is best understood by its opposite face of non-cause/non-effect leading to the dispersion of form and energy, which is what all unaware sentient beings are faced with when passing on. Not recognizing the Pure Mind Path and its life Path as the only true direct means for creating the necessary results of becoming an Eternal Being sets in motion the natural law of no cause, thereby no effect, which results in the dispersion of human form and consciousness.

The Path to Pure Mind gives freedom and liberation creating the karmic energy body of an In-Perpetuum Being, as opposed to other illusionary belief systems which are widely alleged.

Love: Most pain and suffering comes from frustrations which create a great deal of mental stress. The human thinking process, which is strictly dualistic at this point in man's evolution, asks or seeks something in return for its efforts, time, and/or affection. This naturally leads to expectations, and those expectations can be called the root cause of frustration and suffering. Possibly the most glaring example comes from the human's expectations of being "in love." People expect many things both from the person they love and from the act itself. Such expectations and anticipations are based on unfulfilled promises, disappointment, stress, and inevitably some degree of hate. An expectation of love to be returned places the other person in the state of bondage, making love a duty to be discharged, something that must be done. This type of love relationship is never fulfilling because it is not freely given. Bondage is a tremendous burden for one to carry, especially when the cause of it is another person demanding, even begging for love. At this point, there is only resentment. Love originating in a motion or sensory desire dies very quickly, for anything that seemed beautiful about it is lost in unfulfilled expectations. When you love with expectation, you kill it, it is dead. Love cannot exist if there is something you want out of it.

<u>Love is an end unto itself. Loving another is the end. No expectations, no demands, no desires, except to love.</u>

When love is not a give-and-take situation, you can never be frustrated for nothing is expected. On the other hand, people also hope love will end their frustrations of loneliness, sexual desires, etc. Here love as they seek it comes with strings, or again expectations and therefore, it is not a pure emotion but a striking of a bargain, a give-and-take "deal." If you asked nothing in return, you will not have expectations, and therefore, there will be no frustration forthcoming.

When emotions are pure and freely given, man's whole being fills with love; these energies with their pure ecstasy and joy are the very energies man seeks and must create to maintain a previously created eternal energy vessel.

We can find many examples of a fulfilling love in everyday life, that is, where you have the freedom to love openly and fully for you do not have any expectations of it being returned. Unfortunately, these loves are almost exclusively for things that are other than human. You cannot ask for or place a burden (though some try with sentient animals) of expectations upon them. So they have nothing of your expectations to live up to, and they are free to love as they choose.

The simple, pure act of love is a total giving asking nothing in return. Being unconditional, love leaves one free to love anywhere, anytime, and anyone without fear of frustration, disappointment, and suffering.

People, in general, are frustrated. They have ideals and lofty expectations. They live in a society and are expected to conform to their ideals of right and wrong. They formulate a utopian model of life which no one, including themselves, can live up to. They not only expect too much they also expect immediate transformation by themselves as well as by the world. Unfortunately, the world does not take heed and goes on its merry way resulting in more frustration.

The cause or object of frustration makes no difference, but love, power, wealth, religion, and God are the greatest causes. Seeking wealth and/or power creates many expectations and illusions, for these things call for cooperation and bargains with others. Religion is a structure which should release frustration, yet it is a greater cause of it. It proposes to bring you closer to God, so it offers something you seek in return for your devotion. The search for God is probably the most devastating because it is Universal Nature's desire for you to awaken that is the driving force behind that desire and so it is very deep and natural. Therefore, a search for "God" is really a search for Truth but having an Omnipotent being as the object of man's search leads to a wholly misguided quest and more unanswered questions. This God search carried on through meditation, prayer, or any formal religious structure begins with the expectation of finding or knowing, and here again you have the great playing field of suffering. Know that if man stops seeking with expectations, and loves openly and freely asking nothing in return, Truth will come to him, fill him, and be with him, for eternity.

The Path to Pure Mind to Truth and its embodiment may be very difficult indeed, but other paths are impossible. The improbability of logical thinkers stepping beyond their minds limitations to think of the Path's reality as other than fantasy is rampant.

If it had not been part of my awakening to experience the following occurrences, I would probably have come to the same conclusion. For a moment stop and consider that without programmed reincarnation resulting in an eternal being, we still would have no answers. Nevertheless, by refusing to go beyond conditioned logical thinking and a cognitive comfort zone, no matter the present state of spiritual practice, if any, students would disassociate themselves from any further spiritual possibility and any chance of experiencing all the profound truths.

Reawakened In-Perpetuum Beings view with amusement the awe and wonderment shown by those who are in the process of reawakening. Such was the case when I approached them about the authenticity of the following enlightened awakenings. These awakenings were first transmitted to me after my initial reawakening. Some of these phenomenal truths, I had come to learn, and experience in other lifetimes, and were being re-experienced by me in this lifetime. Inspiring experiences leading to awakened Truths are achievable for advanced student practitioners of the Pure Mind Path except for those occurrences dependent on being in a formless state or having been in that state and are presently reincarnated.

My realization that student's success greatly depended on awakening to and accepting the following indisputable Universal Truth because this Truth is the primary premise of Pure Mind practice, and therefore, his success placed intense pressure on my ability to communicate successfully the following enlightened Truths.

Life as An In-Perpetuum Being:

An In-Perpetuum Being/nonbeing flows in and out of life forms thousands of times during any one cycle (the number partially depends on when within a cycle he attains his eternal state). Whether in physical form or not, there is always life, always things happening. To believe that to be in physical form is the only instrumentality for living is ludicrous. All energy is alive, and although it may be dormant at times, it's still very much existent, it's just a matter of whether senses are affecting it or not. A lot of things happen in the break between two physical forms. Senses have no bearing on whether the In-Perpetuum Being is in physical form or not. Having a body form is one means of his existence, and that existence is primarily for experiencing the evolutionary progression of that period of time of whatever, wherever, and through whatever form he chooses to be reincarnated in. As an Earthling, it is only without the interference of body and mind that he finds the spiritual dimensions, so for anyone to believe there is no life beyond body, mind, and senses is to say, "there are no spiritual dimensions to be known or experienced." It would be a travesty to accept energy and spirituality as non-living dimensions. Awareness and consciousness are very much present when we are in a non-being formless form. It's an important part of Universal Nature's need to know itself.

There is also some misconception about time. As long as something is in form, time will exist, although it doesn't exist for that which is not yet to be in form. Since Eternal Beings always exist as an energy form or in some other form, time will exist as the cycle of Universal Life keeps on moving towards its evolutionary end.

There are a substantial number of reasons In-Perpetuum Beings reincarnate to a human form. For instance, as energizing a latent possibility or energizing his energy vessel by rejuvenating and rebuilding his pure energy vessel (energy vessels and their bindings can dissipate, wear down, or be thinned). A lot of energy is lost and/or tarnished while an In-Perpetuum Being is in human sentient form, especially because humans are infantile in their evolution. Until the Perpetual Being begins to turn inward toward spirituality and his reawakening his energy can continue to dissipate.

To answer the obvious question at this point, yes, an In-Perpetuum Being can lose that precious eternal state. It has happened, but not often.

Movement while out of form is by the attraction of energies. In-

Perpetuum Beings are not bound by either time or space and are in constant motion throughout the universe. They are attracted to various stars, planets, or solar systems by energy forces. That's how they're able to visit other species and planets inhabited by sentient or nonsentient life forms. Briefly experiencing life on any planet, while out of a sensory bodily form, is simply a matter of choosing a being who is in the process of creating a great deal of energy (usually of a sexual nature or of similar activity) and entering that being's body along with the new energies that the host is creating. The In-Perpetuum Being's awareness is affected by the host's body's pure senses, but not his mental interpretations.

This practice, I'm sure sounds like fun and can be, but it is also very serious when it comes to choosing future incarnations and definitions. Leaving the host usually takes place while he sleeps. He or she, for the most part, is not aware of any of this, with the possible exception of a very long and intense high from the experience that he was enjoying at the time the energy vessel entered.

After receiving or creating an energy vessel and then passing out of physical form, if a student does not have a reincarnation defined by his teacher, then the student will come back whenever and wherever a human type creature is born. Usually, this takes place in about 100 of Earth's years, but to us, it is measured as less than a blink of an earthling's eye. Once back and reawakened he can choose all his future reincarnations in that universe's cycle. If he chooses to return in a form such as a flower or a bird, he must also choose another reincarnation to follow that one, because he can only define when he is in a form that can think abstractly. If he chooses not to define the reincarnation that will follow after having lived the natural life of an eagle, for example, he'll return sometime as an abstract thinker in some form or another.

An In-Perpetuum Being whose energy vessel is very powerful and plentiful due to his creation and incorporation of pure energies over many aeon's of reincarnation can place dormant energy packets into worthy (defined as the depth of practice and attainment) students' bodies. The amount placed depends on the receiver's mental awareness, life practice, understanding, and potential to maintain the energies. After the receiver passes out of physical form a new In-Perpetuum Being is born. With the new Perpetual Beings traits naturally cleansed and purified, together with the traits of the donor, the vessel is further polarized. This is a thumbnail sketch of a very complicated process, but it is, nevertheless, how it transpires.

To be chosen for transference of an energy vessel enabling the most precious state of eternal being is exceptional. All seekers are first carefully screened as to their potential success in maintaining the state of In-Perpetuum.

The Breath of Universal Nature:
It is the energy that contains, carries, and communicates the essence of Universal Nature. It is this essence of all Truth and wisdom that we awaken through deep meditative practices, and it is that energy (breath) that fills us with moments of ecstasy during the awakening process.

The Breath of Universal Nature is not only subject to constant transformation, but it is at the same time able to make use of various mediums of movement without interrupting its course.

Think of an electric current and how it can flow through copper, iron, or water, and yet how it flashes through space without any medium when the tension is high enough, or how it moves in the form of radio waves.

The Breath of Universal Nature utilizes the blood, nerves, or the breath (inhalation) as conductors and at the same time, moves and acts beyond and without these mediums into the infinity of space. This constant flow naturally moves through all form and space, but it is also at the command of In-Perpetuum Beings when and if, they choose to concentrate it in order to direct this movement.

The Breath of Universal Nature is more than nerve-energy or the vital forces of the blood flow and much more than our breath. It is more than the creative powers of semen or the forces of nerves, more than the faculty of thought and intellect or willpower. All these are just modifications of the Breath.

To experience the Breath of Universal Nature within the human body, we must know and follow its movement through the five layers of human consciousness. The fifth layer, having the greatest density is the physical body built up by nutrition. The fourth is the fine material layer sustained and nourished by the Breath and penetrates the physical body. The third is our thought body, our personality, formed through active conscious thought. The second is the layer of our potential consciousness, which extends much deeper than our active thoughts (subconscious) and comprises the total of our spiritual capacities. The last and finest layer which penetrates all previous ones is the energy essence body (the Breath) of the highest universal consciousness, which we practitioners nourish and sustain in ourselves with our powerful meditative energy and pure high energy emotions of love, kindness, and the exalted joy attained in a high conscious state. This layer is only experienced in the state of enlightenment or the highest stages of meditative awakenings.

These layers are not separate in the human, but rather have the nature of mutually penetrating forms of energy, from the finest all-pervading luminous Breath consciousness to the densest form of materialized consciousness which appears to us as physical bodies. All of these layers work together. At the same time as the physical body is being built through nourishment, it is being penetrated and kept alive by the vital forces of inhalation and exhalation. In the same way, the active thought-consciousness penetrates the breath and helps determine the form of the body will take. Thought, breath, and body are further penetrated and motivated by the still deeper consciousness of experience, intuition, and evolutionary information. Some call this our subconscious.

In the advanced states of meditation, when awakened, all these conscious and subconscious material, vital, and physical functions are further penetrated and transformed into spiritual energy through inspiration and joy until the essence of Universal Nature is revealed and becomes apparent. This is one of the foundations on which rests the Pure Mind Path and its meditative life practice.

It is, therefore, only the spiritual mind/body created by the Pure Mind Path student which penetrates all five layers and thus integrates all his organs and faculties into one complete whole. In this process of integration, of becoming whole and complete, awakened and enlightened, of creating purified energies that dissolve back into themselves and flow into his new vessel, he further evolves into a liberated state of perpetual energy, and in this process lies the secret of immortality.

Those who do not attain this completeness and therefore identify with lesser values, with parts of or partial aspects, are subject to the laws of matter and all its components: the law of mortality. It would, therefore, be a mistake to ignore the value of our physical body, because even though our bodies are by nature limited, insofar as not being able to penetrate the other dimensions the body itself is penetrated by all universal consciousness. It thus becomes the natural stage of all spiritual decisions and movement and is the mediator between self and Self. The spiritualization of meditation, therefore, places the Breath of Universal Nature in this most accessible form for our awakening.

<u>Awakened Energy:</u>

Awakened energy is the only living link that connects us with the hidden forces of our pure natural Self. The concentrated calling up and direction of these forces is the concern and responsibility of reincarnated In-Perpetuum Beings. The evocation of new awakened knowledge and hence the evolutionary movement of the human species towards its final enlightened state is in the hands of reincarnates and their students who are striving to become as such.

Having been asked many times to describe the awakening experience, we always repeat the words, "It is an incident happening in which we truly and completely forget ourselves when experiencing a higher reality. This can only be accomplished through an act of self – surrender which frees and transforms our innermost being. It is an ecstasy that fills us beyond our normal sensory capacities far greater than our prior experiences."

Energy is created by and for the human in many ways, but for our purposes we need to concern ourselves with only five. First, we create a certain amount of energy while we are in a state of rest. Second, we create a great deal of energy through both mental and physical exertion. The amount created is in direct proportion to the effort put out. Third, energy comes with an awakening experience, where the amount and power are directly related to the level or depth of the awakening. There are five levels of awakening, and the highest is the awakening to all Truth; this will usually happen in an immediate and direct manner. Fourth, is energy that we garner from outside. This can come from the rays of the sun, music that flows from natural rhythms, lightning, etc. Lastly, we can receive direct pure energy from an In-

Perpetuum Being.

All positive and pure energy is harnessed by its manifestation in living deeds and its embodiment into the character traits of the student and bound together by the positive emotions of compassion, love, kindness, and Universal Truth's teachings of moral conduct.

The energy that comes from awakening, due to its elevated level of power, is the energy used by "adepts" for things such as levitation, astral travel, and mind over matter demonstrations. But such uses of this energy are a waste of its purpose and are considered a defilement by Perpetual Beings. It is, therefore not practiced as a rule by reincarnates or their students. Unfortunately, we may see these energy vibration games performed by those whose practice is tainted and faulty and whose spiritual life practice is unfulfilled.

When the mind is abiding in silence, it is free from intellect and the human's ever-changing moralistic attachments. A being living in this pure free state is not hampered by senses or dualistic thinking.

<u>**The Final Life Moment and Transcendence to an In-Perpetuum Life Force**</u>:

The Pure Mind practice of energy control and movement are the steps necessary for man's transcendent energy vessel to depart the body through his third eye, not his crown. The practice traditions of the past will eventually be modified to reflect these newly awakened Truths. Modifications may include the understanding of Buddha's Four Noble Truths, impermanence, the Law of cause and effect or karma, and the meaning for life as a human. It is only through the third eye exit that the bindings holding the vessel and its consciousness as one can be polarized. This, along with its successful energizing, is the last step on the Path of becoming an In-Perpetuum Being.

RIGHT LIVING
The embodiment of Truth

Behind all our inspiration and deep awakenings stands that "mysterious" spiritual energy of the Breath of Universal Life, which encourages us to continue on the Pure Mind Path, our chosen life practice, and transforms us as we go beyond until we ourselves have matured into the object of our effort.

Studying In-Perpetuum Beings one will begin to understand more fully the living practice dictated by Universal Nature. Knowing that these types of beings have existed for all time and therefore predate all religion, psychologies, and philosophies, causes one to realize that they have no fixed dogma or religion, but are totally guided by Absolute Truth and the Breath of Universal Life. Through what we might label visions or awakenings, they naturally embody a life practice consistent with Universal Nature's tenants. Their living practice allows them to consciously bridge the chasm created by the human mind between the physical and spiritual worlds.

Perpetual Beings rely on inner knowledge to form conclusions about situations, rather than material or economic concerns which dictate intellectual and, therefore, inevitably wrong conclusions.

As In-Perpetuum Beings flowing in and out of physical form, they are fully aware that all elements of all the environments in and around all of the universes are alive and contain life-sustaining energies. All life forms are interconnected and driven by the Breath of Universal Life. All is dependent and mutually supportive and must be maintained in harmony and good health. Human beings must learn to understand this balance and learn to live in harmony with it, always setting aside ego in favor of all that is natural.

Universal Nature is the source of all power, and the Breath of Universal Life is the source of all Truth. Knowing and living Universal Nature's way is the source of all successful activities.

One-way Perpetual Beings access knowledge is through "awakening journeys." These journeys access the Breath's information by turning deeply inward while focusing on the question or problem. Answers are provided directly or indirectly depending on the degree of the meditative state and purity of mind. This method allows seekers the broader vision of Universal Nature as opposed to the dualistic intellectual mind.

Studying an In-Perpetuum Being is almost impossible unless you are his student. It is said that a student who doesn't understand his teacher's words and possibly more important doesn't understand the teacher's behavior is not a true student. Behavior is many times a better way of expressing one's meaning, clearly better than words. In Pure Mind practice we put an emphasis on behavior, not necessarily how to be, but the natural expression of ones self when you listen to or observe a teacher. You should give up all your subjective opinions; just listen and observe his "way." Listening without saying anything will give you the full meaning of what's being said, implied, or shown. After all, what need be said?

Students embodying Right Living know that with each step forward on this wondrous Pure Mind Path they will rise beyond, for each and every step leads to the fulfillment of Universal Nature's call to awaken in every moment of a student's life comprises (among other things):

--- the personal manifestation of awakened knowledge

--- the avoidance of negative unwholesome factors in the future and the elimination of those which are present

--- wholly selfless giving

--- using the exertion of restraint, of overcoming, of maintaining, of developing the factors of awakening

--- striving to go beyond beliefs and convictions, though they were once of use to you, to Truth

--- continuous Pure Mind meditative practices

--- knowing that beliefs vary according to one's awakenings or lack of.

--- mindfulness/living the present moment with the attitude of a pure spectator through which clear awakenings can be brought forth. The continuous practice of mindfulness brings one's mind under control and

allows one to choose either a state of rest, or states of vision, or states of contemplation, etc., depending on whether one is aiming for awakening or insight into Universal Nature of all existence (one of the basics of enlightenment) or for the creation of pure energy

--- striving to go beyond deceptive "inner experiences"

--- constant effort; showing endurance

--- burning any trace of self in each moment, and leaving no moments unfulfilled

--- not having nor performing any harmful thoughts or actions against any living sentient being

--- the avoidance of actions and thought that conflict with moral conduct dictated by Universal Nature

--- right livelihood, avoiding professions that are harmful to any sentient beings

--- using good deep concentration in all endeavors

--- understanding not to rely on your own opinion, especially when judging your needs

The life practice of a Pure Mind Path student involves much more and goes much deeper than just observing the lofty virtues as previously described. The prime essential is for the student's mental attitude to be solidly based on the recognition of Universal Nature, and they must know or see themselves as Eternal Beings. They must accept the void of the ego, and their thoughts, words, and deeds must reflect these realizations. Practice divorced from the right conduct or practice and the right conduct divorced from the right attitude is totally useless.

One of the ways we live our practice is to study, and one of the most important things we study is ourselves. We look at the makeup of our mind/body, what we think, and how our thought processes work. Through study and practice, we seek freedom, freedom from our fears, anxieties, desires, suffering, frustrations, and the like. We come to know that as we begin to comprehend how our ego minds operate, we can start to forget our ego selves and actually see that we can become the activity of existence or reality itself. When we reach this point satisfactorily, we start to reach for higher meanings beyond our physical existence, towards becoming an Eternal Being. It is also at this point that we truly start to enjoy our sentient existence.

Awareness and awakenings of the spiritual dimensions are an important purpose of the Path. It is designed to make students aware of their every moment so that they can live the meaning of life in their every-day activity as Universal Nature means it to be.

When we begin to understand and live correctly, we will be doing just what we should do. That is all! Nothing more. We awaken when it's time to awaken, we meditate when it is time to meditate, we work when it's time to work, we eat when it's time to eat, and always re-create positive energy. Knowing the purpose of life, we come to understand that our life practice is nothing special, and so we feel nothing special. We just embody our practice, and that is man's initial purpose.

"Outside" people looking at our spirituality, the simplicity of our life, the joy and happiness we radiate have a deep feeling of awe towards us; but those who are practicing do not have that feeling. To us this is just our life; we are just doing what we do, living our life standing there being "normal." Those non-seekers who are fortunate enough to have the time to stop and listen to the wind and feel the sun filtering through the pines always have a deep emotional feeling of awe; a few will possibly write a poem for the occasion. This is the way nature tempts us to follow its guidance.

To have good feelings about our practice is certainly not the point. Our disciplined life practice is not good or bad, hard or easy. We are doing exactly what Universal Nature tells us to do: fulfill our purpose, nothing more and certainly nothing less.

In-Perpetuum Beings move in and out and through levels of consciousness in a flash and at their will. They handle change easily because of their ability to adapt the spiritual as well as ordinary states of consciousness. They are quite comfortable with things that seem unbelievable yet may be true. They are not intellectual philosophers but awakened practitioners. Their knowledge of the Breath of Universal Life and how to communicate with it teaches them how all the energies in the *universe work and how to use them. Recognizing the inherent power of Universal Nature and Absolute Truth and their connection with it manifests in moral behavior. They practice outside of rituals and have no religious articles of worship. Through meditative practices, they have learned how to relax their physical bodies so that they become more receptive and efficient. They are able to quiet their minds so that they can receive and comprehend awakenings. Using tools of imagination when they first start a meditative practice, they are able to envision a journey to various places for the knowledge and vital information necessary to see any evolutionary state in order to qualify other latent possibilities. <u>All visible comes from invisible reality.</u> They show no mystical aura and will not perform "magic tricks." They know how to laugh because they can detach themselves from the human condition and therefore find it amusing. They know not to judge situations or events but just to trust their inner self. They refuse to place any significance on modern-day commentaries of classical texts. They know how to understand people and how to help them towards healing. They also have great insight into all living beings. Their ability to communicate internally as well as externally at the same time keeps them in both worlds simultaneously. They are, therefore, in touch with both and do not lose track of either. They are aware that the human mind is limited in scope and a hindrance to understanding beyond the known to the unknown. They will not produce an atmosphere of power to prove anything. Looking at the life of a Perpetual Being you see the "Way" of Universal Nature manifested by their right living practice.*

In order to teach the elements of a right living practice, we must address the true nature of defilements, attachments, dualistic thinking, and other inner dangers for the purpose of their elimination and or separation. These things provide no true happiness or spiritual gain.

Defilements come from clinging to things, understanding the aggregates of attachment, because if you are successful in separating the aggregates from clinging, you will separate yourself from defilement. The most common aggregates of attachments are: emotion, body, will, memory through perception, and consciousness.

Emotion: Impermanence is easy to forget when pain and pleasure arise. We easily overlook the fact that they are not Self, so we identify with them and thus are tortured by these misunderstandings.

Physical form (body): not accepting aging, decay, and the eventual death of our bodies; our body's constant prey to illness and pain when it is not in harmony with our desires; and when we feel attraction or repulsion towards others, we have grief, sorrow, and we suffer a great deal. One or all of these factors can rob us of any true peace.

Will: The imposing of our preferences. When we do not understand the nature of mental states, we react, sometimes violently, causing our thoughts and feelings, likes and dislikes, happiness and sorrow to arise, and forgetting that they are impermanent and Selfless, we cling to them.

Memories and perceptions: We identify with what we recognize, and this almost always gives rise to hatred, greed, and or delusion. Our wrong perceptions and understandings become habitual, strongly embedded in our subconscious.

When all or any of these attachments are incorrectly understood they lead to the wrong action. A student's goal is to understand and let go of these things so as not to cling to "me or mine." These aggregates of attachments have a potential for great harm and will not disappear, so we must simply not grasp them as our own. Those few who understand the impermanence of these things and practice accordingly will come to know boundless joy.

Attachments, one of the "inner dangers," rob us of our freedom and ultimately destroy us. Our senses bring the things to us that cause lust, anger, compulsion, and cause ignorance to arise. These things have the power to destroy the love, compassion, and kindness within us. Defilements caused by emotion can bury our True Nature beneath insurmountable pile of illusions. Last, but not least, our greed and hatred which continually bring us to anguish; lust and aversion which cause us to speak and do wrong; delusions which lead us to see good as bad, ugly as beautiful, valueless as valuable. *Those who do not live the Pure Mind Path do not see.*

We strive for a practice that is undefiled, and in order to accomplish something even close to that state, we must first eliminate the most pertinent defilements. The defilements which most immediately navigate most of the previously created or gathered energies are: knowingly killing or abusing or causing to be killed or abused any living sentient being either physically, verbally, all with thought projection; any attempt, realized or not, to disrupt the community or its teachers; stealing, lying, gossiping, or any other such deceitful practice. And if one's life practice does not remain well intended and properly interwoven with the conduct and attitudes that constitute the basis of Pure Mind practice, it will bear the consequences of defilement.

AWAKEN THE UNKNOWN

Wisdom being immortal does not die with man, it continues to flow unhindered.

Awakened enlightenment is not something to talk about, but something to manifest in your life.

The deep enlightenment of Universal Nature cannot be described in words, terms of doctrine, and forms of ceremony. Doctrines need only a minor amount of teaching, ritual ceremony needs only obedience and repetition, and words cannot express the two sides of truth, positive and negative, so we cannot express the whole truth in one word.

Universal Nature is something which is in creation itself, not something which results from creation.

Awakenings are expressed by their embodiment and cannot be figured out by logic. Enlightenment is something we express by our activities, our joy, and our enjoyment of the moment.

Awakenings can be very complicated to describe, very simple to experience, and we still find it hard to understand them. Yet understanding enlightenment to any depth becomes rather simple when you practice the Pure Mind Path, and in particular, it's meditation techniques, though these techniques are not enlightenment itself.

Enlightenment cannot be attained by another's words or by conceptualizing. "Be your own lamp." Buddha

Enlightening moments, in which one momentarily awakens to some or all Truths of Universal Nature, are direct and unmediated experiences, almost always attained by those devoted to the Pure Mind Path.

Contrary to widely held belief, enlightenment is not brought about by visions, drugs, hypnosis, ecstasy, voodoo, dancing, whirling, praying, meditation techniques, kundalini, or any other "Paths" claimed by various religions, cults, new agers, and the like.

Awakening Truth lies in total submission of the human will and intellect. The seeker applies rigorous self-discipline in preparation for these "mystical" experiences.

The unanimous descriptions of reincarnate "mystics" such as all Buddha's, Jesus Christ, St. Teresa of Avila, St. John of the Cross, Gandhi, etc., together with the manifest intellect and moral qualities shown by these people make it impossible to doubt or reject this Path to Pure Mind out of hand as mere delusion.

Why would reincarnates choose to live again in any form only to become tainted by that of what forms nature with the possibility of losing the state of In-Perpetuum?

Reincarnates begin to recover their pure integrity with Universal Nature's call to turn back inward. They become purer and purer as they go deeper and deeper beyond their humanity. After they reinvigorate their energy essence vehicle as it was before returning to human form, and when they release from the mind-body and the material world with its perplexities and suffering, Eternal and Perpetual Beings totally recover their pure integrity.

When a student awakens the unknown, he is in a spiritual dimension. Spirituality shines because he has been deeply inspired, touched, and penetrated by Universal Nature's essence. He embodies the universal aspects of reality beyond man's nature, and he characterizes his highest moral quality.

With spiritual awakening, words cannot convey its message. It is a phenomenon that is inexpressible.

When you hear the roar and sounds of creatures, you cannot express the meaning or the feeling of it through words. You can be judgmental, saying it was good or bad, but that doesn't convey anything. As when walking in the desert and seeing a beautiful flower in the midst of arid sands, you can say it is beautiful, but those words will never convey the actual realization of the moment, because they will be interpreted according to the listener's experiences. A person who has never seen nor felt the beauty and the depth of that particular moment might understand the words without understanding anything at all.

Spiritual awakenings are so infinite, so precise and impeccable, so silent that trying to express them in language destroys them. Spiritual things cannot be conveyed, because words cannot fit things into a very narrow sphere and most of their meaning is lost.

Science, physics, and mathematics can be conveyed and therefore taught. But in the realm of ideas and emotions, the more you try to convey the more you feel like your words have left something behind. Like giving someone an empty can, they hold the container without the contents. As a moment between mother and child, how is it possible to convey that feeling to another person?

There is reason which is wholly expressible; there are emotions, and they are expressible to a point beyond which they become inexpressible; and finally, there's spirituality, which is absolutely inexpressible. Spirituality, therefore, cannot be taught.

Awakenings are limitless, so there is no definitive way to end this record, except to say that when a devoted practitioner of Pure Mind practice passes out of physical form, there is his beginning.

Embodying by living the lofty Pure Mind Path the student has cleansed himself of all hindrances through calming his desires, passions, and most importantly negating his ego. The practice opens the heart/mind to the never-ending influx of intuitive wisdom. By advancing onward, the seeker fully experiences the state of consciousness which rises moment by moment and beyond this to the state of pure non-dualistic thought, a oneness with the energies and the essence that flows in and out and around all things.

Reading or hearing words avails one absolutely nothing. It is only the undefiled experience of it that liberates, awakens, and enlightens.

Students who send forth their minds to dwell in silence day after day, night after night, year after year, cease to be as other beings. Their personalities, thoughts, words, and deeds are saturated through and through with the brilliance of non-attachment consciousness as they approach the state of an In-Perpetuum Being. Into them, wisdom flows unhindered. There alone is the honor that comes with this mighty achievement, provided that their thoughts, deeds, and practice remain well intended and properly interwoven with the conduct, attitude, and morality which constitute the Pure Mind Path and Universal Nature.

Awakening experiences are the equivalent of a spiritual education which is not attainable through a structured dictatorial system. In modern-day religions a student is conditioned to confuse many basic premises of spiritual growth. Accepting deceptive premises, he sees himself as learning, because he is being taught; he sees the upward advancement in a church's hierarchy as spiritual attainment; he believes with the publishing of the text he has said or created something new and significant; he sees being educated to perform a service, such as teaching, as having value. These and many more poorly conceived premises are allowed to continue because people have an overwhelming "hunger" for spiritual growth. Religion's basic premises, for the most part, do not incorporate Universal Natures tenets, and therefore cannot begin to fulfill a person's basic desire for spiritual growth beyond simple low-level awakenings.

As a result of a few minor awakenings and multitudinous self-indulgent books, religion is able to justify its existence. It can and often does deceive most of society by claiming as its value its ability to serve man in his search and his attainment of spiritual enlightenment. With the illusion of spiritual advancement, many religions have deceived society into financing its institutions. It is under the guise of spirituality that religion claims freedom from taxation and society's laws. It is while under the protection of these ill-conceived laws that religion allocates more and more of its tax-free dollars to management and facilities, which may be seen as its true underlining purpose given its lack of any true spiritual understanding or practice.

Although a seeker's awakenings can be enhanced and sped up by only a very few religious institutions, nevertheless the seeker's attainment should not be adjudicated by his institution's religious affiliation, it's teachers, religious text, robes of rank, diplomas, rite of passage ceremonies, or dharma transmissions. Every education spiritually inspired or obtained by formal education should be linked and judged by a student's embodiment and practice of that education. Most certainly, spiritual growth should not and cannot be judged by symbols attainable by approved and/or condoned measures under religions or society's control.

ENERGY IN RELATION TO MOTION AND SPACE

A sentient being exists in a three-dimensional form, with sense perception, and thought both memory and abstract, and in this category is human. The nature of space, however, is not limited to three dimensions: it includes all possibilities of movement, not only the physical and mental, but also the spiritual movement which comprises infinite dimensions. Turning inward to the spiritual dimensions will put a human on a much higher plane of existence. The Earthly human being is in an infancy phase of his evolution which makes it difficult to recognize and/or understand the spirituality dimension of which he is capable.

This plane of spiritual activity is called "the spiritual dimension of consciousness." When one reaches the highest degree of this consciousness, a state where the duality of object and subject is eliminated, he enters the Universal Nature Dimension. This state of awareness goes beyond the human and all other natures that are tied to behavior and form.

The principle of movement can only be understood by knowing its prime mover which the Breath of Universal Life is. This Breath is the all-powerful, all-pervading rhythm of Universal Nature which directs the course of all things in every dimension. The interaction of body and mind, of spiritual and material forces, of matter and consciousness, sense organs and sense objects, are totally dependent upon the Universal Life Breath to function. Without it, that interaction would be impossible. It is precisely this interaction which we make use of, and upon where the techniques of our Pure Mind meditation is grounded.

The body and mind are the instruments we have for the awakening of Universal Nature. Any turning away from this physical life is a turning away from the completeness of Universal Nature's Wisdom and a renunciation of its aim in an earthly human embodiment. Therefore, we must not ignore the body and mind for they are indispensable to a perfect spirituality and the achievement of an In-Perpetuum state.

Frequently Asked Questions

Most questions asked of enlightened beings and of oneself are nonsense. Intellectual and metaphysical questions are for verbal knowledge, not for authentic practice and living. One should ask questions that lead to or are concerned with the spiritual and inner dimensions. The intellect is our connection to the outside, to the material world. So, answers to such questions never lead to the inner spiritual dimensions nor provide anything meaningful in helping one become a Perpetual Being.

Questions and answers can become a vicious cycle, always spinning on the periphery; the heart is never reached. Have you ever noticed that most questions ask about something, especially about self, but knowing about yourself is not knowing you, so you gather much knowledge about things and never truly know or experience them or your true Self.

When you choose to ask a question, ask one that will aid in deepening your practice for this is what your future and present lives depend upon. Try to ask questions that are of the very moment you are in; ask a "now" question. When you ask such a question, it is a step towards personal freedom. Furthermore, questions whose answers will not change you in any way are meaningless for example: how many planets throughout the universe support sentient life? What difference will the answer make to you? How will the answer change your life or help you with your practice, on the other hand, if the answers you seek will change you or your practice, then they become very meaningful. Questions should also come from the immediate moment, spontaneously. If no questions arise and all you feel is deeply silent, that is ideal. Alas, only a few who question and study truly want to practice. Most want to study and know in an intellectual way. This is totally meaningless in a spiritual practice of importance. So, let us move on to the questions I have been asked many times by seekers and students alike.

Most modern-day religions have an approximate date of "birth." How old is the Pure Mind Path of which you speak?

Prior to the practice itself making an appearance here on earth, In-Perpetuum life forces either existed in a form other than human or visited through the means of animal forms throughout the universe. Years after combining evolutionary forces the human species on Earth was created as we know it today. The first Perpetual Being that was reincarnated as a human on this planet turned inward to reawaken the Pure Mind practice, as it is called today. Recognize that the practice has been in existence for many billions of years, and though the practice itself has undergone many name changes, it remains basically the same. Because this practice is under the direct guidance of Universal Nature, it will remain unblemished throughout all universal cycles. It can be no other way.

This practice has appeared in many forms, in all countries, and deep within some religions. Those reincarnates who turned to a religious practice as a means of reawakening transcended that religion's boundaries in short order. Through their enlightenment experiences, they were able to identify the one true practice. Perpetual Beings are and were few in number. They are of all races, faiths, and most live in this world unrecognized by those who do not see, and yet all of humanity is affected by their work and powerful presence.

Are there other means I can consult on the subject of becoming an Eternal Being?

To begin with, we are at a point in the Universal Cycles' wherein energizing of a greater number of latent possibilities is taking place; therefore, an almost doubling of the percentage of all Eternal Beings must also take place. This will require, in Earth's time, quite an extended period, but in comparison to the time/space reality, it's just a blink of an eye. The human species on this planet is involved only to the point where their conscious mind makes it difficult, if not nearly impossible, to awaken deeply and transcend the known. With the keys of Pure Mind Practice and their manifestation, it becomes a matter of doing, being, and receiving. There are relatively few Eternal Beings especially teachers/guides in physical form on Earth. Attracting one depends greatly upon your level of practice and pure energy that can invoke the law of attraction.

If teachers/guides are so crucial, why are they not readily available to most seekers?

Eternal Beings in physical form carryout many functions of evolutionary "shifts" or corrections. Most do not have teaching as a mission. Those who do carry a mission of teaching are not available to just any seeker. A true seeker must have obtained enough purified energy to attract, through the Law of Attraction, an Eternal Being.

What is the Universal Cycle?

Everything within the universe, including the universe itself, begins and ends. To try and picture the Universal Cycle it is best to start at its ending. One moment just before the cycle ends, all physical and thought phenomena that have existed and evolved come to their natural passing. There remains nothing of the possibility that has not been or is not at the present time existing. All have been energized into existence. Along with the human being which has evolved to its final highly spiritual stage, most possibilities have come and gone and are completely known by Existence and Universal Nature. At this point everything comes to its natural end, dissipates, and nothing remains, not even the memory of all that existed, for this moment there is no mind with remembrances. ***The one vital exception is a single In-Perpetuum Being submerged in a myriad of latent possibilities sharing with Universal Nature but one thought, that of knowing their natures, their physical embodiment, their evolution, etc., and most important the understanding that Universal Nature permeates all things***. And so, with the energizing of one possibility, the cycle starts over. Each new cycle brings with it no predestined plan or map to follow. All of them evolve differently from previous cycles, but they have the same tendencies so that they parallel each other closely.

Can you explain the similarity of near-death experiences that people claim to have had?

The descriptions I have read or heard are very close to the actual events of passing out of physical form, though there is a monumental difference between the passing of an Eternal Being and the rest of humanity. As Eternal Beings die, their energies remain intact in what has been called throughout this record their energy vessel. The rest of humanity's energies just release from their cells and flow out through one or all of the nine points of exit spreading throughout the universe. This, of course, includes the mind's energies stored as memory as life slips away, the memory energies leave the cells and occasionally present humans with a very quick glimpse of their whole lives. This is the reason people say, "our whole life passed before us." Their fond remembrances of other people and experiences naturally contain the strongest energies.

For the Eternal Being, his energy vessel continues to gather near what Western science calls the "mysterious gland" and what most mystics, adepts, etc. from the East know as the "third eye." As his energy gathers it gets brighter and brighter until he reaches a point of brilliant white light. When their mind/body ceases functioning, their bound energy vessel leaves the body intact, and the "third eye" which is still functioning, sees this important event recalling that person's life, in its usual spectator role.

The rest of humanity's third eye with its bright light first awakens at this juncture and observes their energies departure. If their mind/body starts to function again, or as people might say "returns to life," then the energy package is forced to reverse and is drawn back through the third eye gland. It is here we find the explanation of "I found myself walking towards a bright light." Actually, it was inward, but there is no way for the mind to know that.

How should humans judge the meaning of their lives?

Almost all humans conduct and judge their lives only as their lives are seen by others. They dress, think, talk, and live in accordance with their society, parents, peers, and desires. Without other people to judge by or to be judged by, they would have no egos, no identity, for what would they identify with? Without something to relate to there could be no color, no race, no gender, no good, no evil, no style, no fat nor thin, no civilization, no laws, no standards, no need for Gods; we would just appear and disappear. There would be no judgment and, in people's eyes, no meaning.

One of the secondary forces that drive human sentient beings to the Pure Mind practice is the search for a meaningful life beyond the judgment of other people. With the awakening to the Truth of impermanence, they begin to understand that all form is transitory including themselves.

Moment to moment nothing remains as it was, nor as one would have it be. Neither our eyes nor our minds can see or know the momentary changes as they take place. Do you see each and every hair on your head turning gray, in fact, your hair, your blood cells, your thoughts, and all other physical aggregates that make up your being and everything else throughout the entire universe are never the same from one moment to the next. So, humans may begin to see that they are not the same person at this moment as they were a moment ago. A person's life, if it is to be judged, can only be judged on a momentary basis. Unless one turns inward, for whatever reason, life just comes and goes, and it's only in the minds of the people they left behind that their life had meaning. It is very hard on the ego to accept that our lives only have meaning based on the judgment of other humans. Unfortunately, ego desire is the wrong reason to turn inward for meaning and therefore can never succeed.

Isn't my nature different from yours? If not, how do you understand the word nature?

Basically, I use the word nature in two diverse ways. First, Nature is the principal and/or power that dictates and guides the natural Essence of Existence for all phenomena and its creation, as in Universal Nature. Second, individual natures are the overall system or pattern of particular objects or forces such as solar systems, planets, humans, animals, plants, etc. as in human nature.

Humans tend to use nature as a rationalization for their behavior. It is never their nature to do something that is in direct violation of Universal Nature's laws. It is because it is their nature to have choices that they are able to create or accept many flaws in their thinking and character. Unfortunately, they see these differences as each one's own nature. There is no question that each sentient being has its own idiosyncrasies, talents, and abilities. However, a human's nature itself does not occur at random; it is the nature of humanity.

Character traits much like belief systems are knowingly or not created or adopted. When correctly understood by man, a tree is a tree, a bird a bird, and a Universal Truth is Truth beyond his definition. Using trees as an example, we can see how they differ one from the other even within the same species. Looking deeper we can see that even on the same tree each leaf is different in color, shape, and size, but each stem from the same root, and like all humans who stem from the same root nature, that nature is permeated by Universal Nature and that Nature cannot change.

As a student evolves, his clarity of seeing will evolve, and his purpose of being and the laws of all Natures will become known to him. As this is happening, he will make fewer and fewer wrong decisions that affect him, the planet, and the universe.

Other than the obvious long-term benefits of the Pure Mind Practice are there any advantages in my present life?

There are many, starting with the realization that you are in charge of your life and can throw away the "victim of circumstances" attitude that most people have. You might even feel inspired by obstacles that you were previously incapable of handling, but now you're capable of doing so. You'll have the capability of tapping into universal energies. Your thoughts about how events in your life are shaped will change. For example, your thinking about linear time will be altered, providing you with much more freedom. Your understanding of the real powers that exist will help enhance your experiences. Your insight into compassion will put your relationships on a far different level, and your communication skills will improve. You will begin to understand how you are connected to all life. No longer feeling separate, your perspective broadens. You will understand how to be in touch with the knowledge you didn't think possible. You will undergo radical transformation the closer you get to the true Nature of Reality. You will become more relaxed and have virtually no stress especially in the face of perceived adversity. You will learn never to allow the events in your life to bind you, but also not to withdraw from them. You will come to think tomorrow's thoughts when tomorrow comes. You will know, understand, and appreciate that worldly feelings are not sublime.

Turning inward, are there materialistic or other things one must have to discard?

Living simply without the burden of possessions might be necessary, but the major things we must all give up or let go of are our ego and our dualistic way of thinking. Thinking unrealistically and egotistically keeps us separate from everything else that exists. When you give up the idea of separateness, there is no distinction between man and woman, sky and earth, teacher and disciple, etc., and you find the true meaning of life. You make no value judgments, because everything has the same value, so when your senses come into contact with something, it is just as it is, nothing more or less. You give each thing the same respect by understanding that all are the same.

Not feeling separate is a very serious part of the Pure Mind Practice and very necessary for a successful conclusion. Not seen as separate from the rest of nature, you begin to realize true knowledge and evoke deep awakenings. At best, the elimination of self-centered ideas is difficult, but the effort will help appease you in the desire to awaken. A true Pure Mind Path student embraces the whole of the universes without labels. The delight of being in union with Universal Nature is sweeter than any material riches or fulfilled desires.

Are teachers and prophets of other disciplines and/or religions likely to be reincarnate's?

These prophets, seers, teachers, gurus, ministers, priests, etc., can become eternal only if their practice recognizes and encompasses all that is dictated by Universal Nature and thereby attracts an Eternal Being. Otherwise, they will continue to live only in the minds, hearts, and words of their students. As with most of humanity, their physical and mental energies disperse upon their passing. In contrast, In-Perpetuum reincarnates live eternal and infinite lives. Their lives are sustained by their deeds, thoughts, and reawakening practice which are solely guided by Universal Nature. Their Pure Mind Practice congeals their energy with all that's infinite. Their everyday deeds, teachings, and their correction adjustments of an evolutionary tract can be seen wherever you look and will be understood whenever you raise your consciousness.

Meeting a teacher of the Pure Mind Practice what should one's aim be?

If and when you meet a reincarnate teacher, try to see what cannot be seen, hear their unspoken words, and try to experience with them the elation of awakening, the revelation of Universal Nature, the inspiration of awe, selfless giving, and unconditional love. This teacher is a guide on the Path of high consciousness, liberation, compassion, patience, unconditional love, and is the one true source of pure practice in human form. Unify your mind with theirs, and you'll achieve and receive.

If after studying with the teacher for a while, he/she were to pass on, who will guide my practice?

If your mirror's dirt has been removed and the dust has settled, the images will remain clear. If your heart is pure, then all things in your world will be pure, then the sun, the moon, the trees, the flowers, as well as the birds and animals will guide you along the way. If this is not the case and you are worthy of the practice another teacher might be attracted to you.

Be grateful to one who urges you to return to your difficult spiritual practice, no matter what their motivation seems to be. Most others offer comfort and an easy Path, and it is those you must worry about.

I have become totally confused with the use of the word enlightenment; can you clarify its meaning?

Enlightenment is a spiritual state of awakening. Unfortunately, there are no words to describe this ungraspable experience. Trying to reduce to words what is conceptually impossible to the human mind is laughable, at best. Enlightenment is not a concept. When experiencing it, there is no separation; therefore there is no object to see nor subject to experience. Where the word enlightenment is used in the sutras and commentaries, it should be viewed as a shallow experience that needs to grow deeper. Enlightenment is a word mainly used to impress others. The more words used to describe and embellish the experience, the more you can believe that the speaker has never experienced it.

You must be aware of the intellectual approach of those who hang on to words and ask you to believe in those words rather than guiding you to experience their deeper meaning directly. Due to the workings of the human mind at this stage in evolution, they can only communicate the relative truths of the phenomenal world or their delusions in opposition to Universal Nature's Ultimate Truth which can be experienced and then communicated in a spiritual dimension.

Most of the hierarchy in the popular world religions are very exposed, very available. Why do In-Perpetuum Beings conceal themselves?

Anyone who is open to the highest spiritual dimensions becomes aware of us and recognizes the spiritual energy that emanates from our presence. Many mystics function secretly. Some seek isolation, away from the "maddening crowd." But whether they go into the mountains, monasteries, forests or caves, their silence is telling, their energies are highly visible, and their work easily recognized. But most seekers are not open, and their awareness level is low. However, the true answer would be, what would be the point? We are not trying to convert or to convince anyone.

You have said many times that logical thought is a barrier to contact with the spiritual dimensions and understandings. Can you give me an example of this?

Logic dictates that one cannot be the many and the one at the same time or vice versa, but while in a spiritual dimension one experiences clearly, and in no uncertain terms that the one is multi-form while remaining one. Applying many different contradictory levels of awakened knowledge to a singular event, experience, or being, can be made very apparent. There are times when it is convenient to view things as independent, other times as an illusion, and yet other times when it is best to recognize them as a void. Logic is useless in the attempt to reach a spiritual state or in spiritual affairs.

Can you express to me in words your experiences and feelings about the Pure Mind Path's Life Practice?

Impossible! But it can be described through the eyes of a student of mine. "The Pure Mind Path is a very deep and undefiled practice which is the perfection of all that (Universal Nature) which is truly perfect. Our life itself is a wondrous practice that is most rare, and for the first time, it is being revealed to all, thereby solving for us the previously hidden and profoundest mystery of all awakened ones. It guides us to the "nowness" of our need to awaken, thereby enabling us to comprehend the Truth of Universal Nature, and it's need for us to become an Eternal Being. It also shows us that there is no other holy awakened life than the Pure Mind Path way of living."

This life practice dictated by Universal Nature is a pure and wondrous way of being and becoming. When being in a joyous serene silence, awakening the qualities of Universal Nature, and further manifesting them by our deeds and thoughts, we reach our union with all things, all natures, and ourselves. Experiencing and understanding the true meaning of life, and the fact that it has merit, and we as humans can indeed play a key role in the universal scheme if we choose to, is a momentous realization moment. We learn that eternal life or eternal nothingness is in our choosing and this energizes us to stay with our practice moment by moment, day by day, year by year, eon by eon. By being on the true Path of the Universal Nature way, we know to **live our whole lives as our practice and not just to fit our practice somewhere in our lives.**

Pure Mind practice also teaches us to be very patient; after cultivating our minds and planting the seeds, we leave the matter of our awakening to the nature of the Breath of Universal Life, for there is nothing else we can do. We understand that we cannot dictate to any nature, so if it takes one or 100 years to awaken fully, we are at peace and do not suffer from expectation.

You speak of different energy groups. Do any of these fall into what people refer to as the spirit world?

Energy underlies all life. What I believe people are referring to is our contact with spiritual energy that is the source for all life and is directly related to each form's nature. Ordinary people see the world as a physical environment that operates according to physical laws, with a certain order, but no meaning. For the Perpetual Being, as well as advanced students of the Pure Mind Path, the Universal Breath of Life, which carries Universal Nature's energy, proves the coherency of all forms and gives meaning to life. Without the greater universal energy, there would be chaos. The Breath's energy is not a theory or a figure of speech but a definite reality that is as fundamental as breathing or thinking. For students, the awakening knowledge of this energy power propels them into mastery of their lives. Understanding the physical world of form and its energies is a good mental exercise but is in no way adequate for understanding our underlying Nature and therefore, does not provide the keys that are essential to truly understanding anything spiritual.

The Universal Breath remains hidden to all people until they unveil it. Having done so, the wisdom beyond all known wisdom and the energy powers become available and clear to them. But like most jewels, they are difficult to unveil, and it may take a very long time to do so. If a student keeps "polishing his mirror," he removes the crust and dust, and lo and behold a jewel is found.

Consider where the In-Perpetuum Being's mind goes to see this knowledge. To the un-awakened when you see a rock, it's a rock, the wind is moving air, animals are sentient beings, and humans are the same with higher mental abilities and emotions. Living or not, when you dissect the human or all other forms, they are just smaller pieces of the same. Take them down further, and they are atoms made up of the same basic materials as all other forms. Go further still, and they are particle waves mostly in what we call "space smoke." At this level science becomes totally confused, having no understanding within and beyond the subatomic level. This is where we spend most of "our" time. Here is where the same underlying universal energy that is within all animals, humans, rocks, trees, wind, water, and all other forms both animate and inanimate reside. Here also is where we can communicate with the Breath of Universal Nature and all other species and forms. It is here that one gains a deep understanding and respect for Universal Nature as well as the ever-evolving natures of all things. Real power comes from knowledge, and that is why it is not available to ordinary people who have no respect for the workings of Universal Nature.

Having heard the expression "clear seeing" as a way to understand "suchness or itness," could you explain it further?

There are so many phrases and words used in attempts to communicate mindful or awakening experiences. We use the phrase "as-it-isness" in our attempt to communicate seeing a thing clearly, or our "oneness" experience with that thing. When you look at something or someone and really see all there is to see, and then it sees you in the same manner. It is at this juncture that it is no longer just it, and you are no longer just you. You and it dissolve into something way beyond words that can be explained logically, but we definitely experience it. To bring about a perfect union this intuitive wisdom requires opening ourselves up and being mindful at the same time. That is clear seeing. But if you attempt to bring any selfish motives to the experience, it will not work.

Awakenings, how do they come about?

Never try to hurry your thought process. For example: Meditation is like watering dry soil; it takes time to seep in and the roots to grow. Awakening is the natural effect of your cumulative efforts. Therefore, it is best never to stop trying. Whether awakenings come quickly or slowly, they will come, but you cannot force them. As with the tree sapling you planted, it will grow in its own time. Your job is to dig the hole, water and fertilize the tree, then protect it as best you can. That much is your part, but the way and time it takes to grow is the tree's affair stemming from its True

Nature. It comes down to this: just practice in the right way with the right attitude, conduct, effort, and leave awakening to Universal Nature. Do this, and you will also be at peace with your practice.

"The faltering student is the one whose eyes are fixed upon the heavens because his feet are stuck in the mud."

Unknown. It is the guide or teacher who recognizes your mired state and lifts you out of the mud to be once again on your joyful way.

Have you had a student who has failed, and if so, what were the reasons?

Yes! The reasons are many, but possibly the overriding reasons were their inability to see the practice as anything but an ordeal, and inconvenience, and their lack of understanding the necessity to get beyond their own desires. Without the patience to pass through their desires, they remain in the category of a person of sensations and not of the spirit. So, they remain today on the suffering level of those who imagine that worldly feelings, especially desire, are sublime.

How does the Pure Mind Path differ from most disciplines and religions that expect a herd mentality from their students?

There is only one Pure Mind Path, and the heart of it is so very simple. That said, it should be added that with this practice no two to students experience their Paths in the same way. Each student's Path has its own characteristics according to his individual walls. The teaching Path twists and turns in response to the particular events the person must experience to allow him to break those walls.

Experience shows that the majority of students spend most of their time understanding and evaluating differences between their aggregate self, and their self-nature. Their greatest and possibly most difficult of all t tasks, is recognizing and setting aside their illusionary moments which are governed by their senses and interpreted by their egos, nature, and Universal Nature or their true Self. The greatest and hardest task is in recognizing and setting aside their illusionary moments which are governed by their senses and interpreted by their egos and focusing on their moments of awakened clarity reached while striving for eternal life, these moments being governed by

Universal Nature. Pure Mind goes far beyond any other practice in its awakened and stated reasons for existence and necessary complexity of practice. On the other hand, it does not share the views of those who insist on rituals or "old-time religion" for the sake of conformity.

Emptiness is a concept I find hard to understand. Will you comment on its value?

For most students reaching the understanding of emptiness proves to be their first momentous awakening. Sorrow, happiness, pain, love, hate, competitiveness, expectation, desire, and many other states or emotions have no basic nature of their own except what we give to them. Therefore, we call them empty. Recognizing our own minds as their source, we also recognize their impermanence, so when they arise, we can let them pass by and not attach to them, thus avoiding most causes of suffering. "The emptier you become, the fuller you get."

In what form will an In-Perpetuum Being reveal himself?

They will appear like any other human that is a prisoner in this world of forms, but unlike them, his form and consciousness can be set aside. Thankfully, this freedom decisively outweighs his imprisonment. If you study them carefully, they will appear to have two centers of consciousness, one human and one not. He may speak from one in any moment and from the other in the next. This accounts for any apparent contradiction one may envision. Whether speaking from one consciousness or the other his words and actions will never conflict with Universal Truth. The highest form of consciousness is not seeing dark or light, you and me, but instead recognizing that your mind is what defines these differences and all relationships. The relationship between a student and his teacher is also this way.

How do you answer the people who insist that each person must find their own way?

In modern day society, it is fashionable to stress freedom to choose a Path to one's awakening. This is most unfortunate because those who speak do not reveal (because they obviously do not know) the true meaning of freedom or how one should go about choosing their Path. Today's other very popular thesis is that "Each person will or must find his own correct Path."

This is simply ridiculous! Through cultural conditioning, humans have come to believe that **"what they like is what they need."** They take apart a proven discipline and pick what conforms to their mental and/or physical comfort zone and call it their Path. If they cannot find anything existing that fits their preconceptions, they feel free to change another's philosophical tenants or invent the practice that does fit. Today, due to humanity's place in its evolution man needs an awakened being to arrange and implement circumstances that would lead him to knowledge and awakening experiences.

What do you feel is the greatest difference in the approach of a Pure Mind student and those of other practices or religions?

Surrender and consumption! In all spiritual, religious, living, and sexual pursuits, a deep and fulfilling climax can only be brought to fruition by surrendering your ego and fears to allow these experiences to consume you. In almost all cases men try to dictate their needs and desires into the practice of love, life, learning, religion and/or spirituality. They spend most of their newfound passion on consuming that which they desire. This way of being without question always results in failure. Spirituality, love, life, etc., offers so much more to man that man can offer to them. The absolute and only way to succeed in these pursuits is for you to surrender totally to whatever you are doing and allow it to consume you fully. Recognize your hunger, so that you may satisfy its craving.

The desire to learn for the purpose of quenching your "hungry ghost" is your test!

All that you have said is very exciting and different but how can I know that is true?

Don't ask us, ask yourself. I and other awakened beings have spoken, and so you have heard or read the Truth. But hopefully, as you have learned this is not the way to understand or to know anything. You must seek your answers beyond yourself from yourself. When Your Mind practice has prepared you for understanding, then in its time, the answers will come, and you will awaken to experience for yourself and know that the Truth is as we have said. No other discipline or religion can prove or state that as a certainty.

How do you explain most of the world's beliefs in a God or Gods?

Whether you use your own criteria or accept someone else's definition of God, there are and always were reasons for Gods coming into being. In most religions, as well as in personal definitions, it is as "the" creator. This is the perfect role for humanity to assign to their conception of God, for now, we have the opportunity to laden God with what should be our responsibilities. "He is the one" responsible for all creation, and therefore, God must take responsibility for all that takes place within it. All the good, all the evil, all the suffering, and all the consequences. Since we place God in a constant state of awareness and doing, we can ask God to alter conditions for our benefit, relief, and comfort.

A God is the perfect scapegoat for all our actions or inactions, the one "somebody" who is ultimately to blame, and yet we must not be too harsh for God is the one who can change the outcome, and so through our prayers, we implore God to do so. For example: when a participant in some sport gets down on his knees and gives thanks to the Lord for his victory, does he really believe that God made a choice between him and his opponent? How did God choose? Was God keeping score on past deeds or prayers? Was the game played on a Sunday, and did God have the day off in order to watch the game? It seems that we place a very large burden of chores and choices on God's shoulders.

In many ways, we are led to believe, either by our own needs or the wishes of others, that God is the creator of all reality, the realities of every day fortunes, misfortunes, births and deaths, happiness and sorrow. If this is true, then how can God be reality itself? Did he create himself? Of course not, for if God was created, then that means God is not God. He is a thing, a word thing that man created to give himself answers, answers which otherwise are seemingly beyond his capability of knowing.

This word God has no connection to any form or reality. It is an illusion resting on the incorrect interpretation of reality. That reality is man's need to fulfill Universal Nature's law of awakening for when nothing is awakened, nothing can be manifested, and therefore nothing can be known.

People are fond of an effortless way to think and live so are not capable of living a practice aimed at awakening, and so they choose easy answers, illusions based on belief systems without any basis in reality. In other words, they choose to believe in a mysterious, unknowable, sometimes benevolent and, all-powerful "God."

Did you ever notice that the hierarchy of all religions talk of God speaking through them or directly to them? They are, therefore, only responsible to God and are not accountable for their actions or the consequences. That they can only be held responsible by God, not by you or by me, is their ego's saving face. No responsibility, therefore no judgment, which is their shelter. It is no wonder that governments, corporations, churches, and other power structures adopt this "somebody other than me" umbrella to operate under.

If you truly need God in your life, then say that God is the essence of all things. A God cannot be a person or thing, for a God cannot be an "it." He would have to be the sum, the totality of itself. Those who call this itness God need a divine, all-powerful form that they can envision and turn to for universal answers and also help solve problems they themselves cannot. With seemingly no other place to turn, humans created God illusions which they hold as separate from themselves.

Totality is indefinable because definition requires a drawing of boundaries, and the totality has no limits; it is infinite. **Man cannot conceive of the infinite for whatever is conceived by mind is limited, finite**. We cannot picture an existence without boundaries, but it is so, and whether we can see it or not makes no difference.

The logical mind demands definition and clearly defined limits. This is why most of humanity cannot reach what lies beyond the known. Those who choose to know God, unfortunately, become disillusioned having chosen to accept a man-made definition. Our languages are not meant to express the indefinable, so don't try!

If Jesus Christ is not the Son of God, did he exist, and if so, who was he?

I will start with the Nag Hammadi Codices. In them, it appears that there were many other "saviors" to descend upon this Earth.

Mithras, the Persian sun god, came from heaven and was born as a man to redeem humanity from its sins. He was also born of a virgin on December 25th, and it was shepherds who first learned of his birth. He too had a last supper with his disciples and then ascended into heaven.

The Egyptian God Horus was another "savior of mankind."Born to Isis, a virgin, seventeen hundred years before Christ. She had an annunciation when a spirit descended, and she conceived when a symbol of life was put to her lips. Isis was also worshipped with the familiar name of the Immaculate Virgin.

Virgin mothers of gods are found in China and Mexico, among Etruscans and Scandinavians. In Greece, January (later as Epiphany by the Christians) was the date the virgin goddess Kore gave birth to Dionysus, whose name was sometimes Les and sometimes Jesus. Krishna was born of a virgin. Even the birth of Caesar Augustus was described by sycophants of his day (writing at the time of Christ's birth) in words almost identical to that used in the Bible: "savior of the whole human race," destined to bring "peace on Earth."

Jesus of Nazareth, later to be known as The Anointed, and The Jewish Messiah, was a reincarnate, a child of Mary and Joseph. Twice spoken of in the New Testament until the age of seven, he disappears for about 23 years and reappears at the age of 30, to become John the Baptist's handpicked disciple and carried on his work. Jesus' ministry lasted for approximately three years until his crucifixion when he was believed to have been resurrected.

Neither the Christian Bible nor Christianity itself has anything to say about his life from the age of seven to the age of 30 or so, his awakening, or how and where he was taught. Where did he disappear to after he was seen by as many as eight different people walking the streets a few days after his "resurrection rising to the kingdom of heaven"?

By preaching mainly to the uneducated masses in words whose meanings they could not relate to, Jesus left everything he said up to interpretation by a materialistic people who had no experience with the spiritual dimensions. Therefore, the words he spoke took on the meaning completely different from what he intended. Confusion and misinterpretations become truth by people whose only perspectives came from dualistic thinking and an exceedingly vengeful God. One of his greatest miscalculations involved the apostles he chose. Having been selected to communicate his teachings, they further misconstrued his already poorly understood words. They were an uneducated, simple people whose burden it was to spread ideas they themselves could not comprehend. In trying to fulfill the Jewish prophecy of a Messiah who would redeem our sins and relieve our suffering, the people and then the church hierarchy have, in fact, created a greater quantity of both.

It is one thing for a man to be a great orator but another thing entirely when the words he speaks are wantonly construed to fulfill the prophecy that people desperately wanted fulfilled.

For the Jews, either Jesus died, and the miracle of resurrection took place, or the whole newly founded religion died. The prophecy called for the coming of Christ, his crucifixion, and further resurrection. If this was not done, then the Jews neither would nor could have believed in Jesus either as a Christ or as a prophet. They never recognized the man who was always attempting meditation because he was struggling to deepen his enlightenment, nor did they recognize a teacher who was preaching to those who were not at all philosophical, spiritually illiterate, and totally literal.

There is much written in the East explaining what seemed to be the "death" of Jesus on the cross. You can read about these mystical arts, that Jesus mastered in the missing years of his life, in many Eastern texts.

Needing the followers of Jesus to believe he was healed and resurrected, the Essenes helped Jesus recover from his wounds during the three days he remained in the cave. When he was healed, he disappeared. It was this disappearance that led to the belief in his resurrection and ascension to heaven.

Jesus eventually resettled in Kashmir where he lived in human form until he was 100+ years old. The whole Arabic world called him Esua. In Kashmir, he is and was known as Yousa-Asaf. His tomb, which can still be seen today, there is his name, footprint, and a plaque proclaiming his arrival in Kashmir. In today's calendar, it loosely translates to the year three C.E.

The whole Judaea fiasco changed the way Jesus lived forever. From then on, he lived in Kashmir continually for approximately 70 years. He did not travel, and he did not preach. He was not seen as a prophet, priest, or minister. Instead, he lived with a small group of awakened beings, worked, and studied silently. He was turning inward to the spiritual dimensions in search of much deeper enlightenment and the strengthening of his energy vessel that he had lost much of during the years in Judea. This esoteric tradition lives today and remains well hidden.

The Dead Sea Scrolls, originally written and preserved by the Essenes, as well as the Koran, are more accurate than the Old and New Testaments of today. They tell a much different version than the writers of the Bible. The Christian hierarchy will not compromise its tenets, because today's Christianity is exoteric and only concerned with the outer materialistic world. It is always the way of exoteric thinkers to wear down and then destroy everything that is esoteric, therefore, a disturbing threat to materialism.

It is correct to believe in Jesus if you leave out Christianity and the written word. You could enrich your understanding if and when you view him as he truly was, a reincarnated In-Perpetuum Being who until he returned to Kashmir, was only somewhat reawakened.

I have heard many different tales of Mary Magdalene, the Virgin Mary, and various other females of historical note. Will you speak about the knowledge you have about them?

The Mary Magdalene found in sources like the Gospel of Philip depict her as being closer to Jesus than any other of his disciples. The closeness described in these writings portrays Mary Magdalene as understanding Jesus and his teaching while the other disciples did not.

Mary Magdalene appears with more frequency than other women in the canonical Gospels where she is again spoken of as being a close follower of Jesus. Her presence at the crucifixion and Jesus' tomb, while hardly conclusive, is at least consistent with the role of grieving widow or dedicated student.

In the book of Luke, there is the story of an exorcism performed on Mary Magdalene that cast out seven demons. She along with Salome, and Mother Mary "had all been healed of evil spirits and infirmities." They later accompanied Jesus on his last journey to Jerusalem; as found in the books of Matthew, Mark, and Luke. Beyond these references in the Gospel narrative and what may be inferred from them, nothing is known of Salome, though some writers conjecture more or less plausible that she is the sister of the

Blessed Virgin mentioned in John.

Mary Magdalene remained at the site of the crucifixion until the body was taken down and laid in a tomb prepared for Joseph of Arimathea. In the early dawn of the first day of the week Salome, Mary the mother of Jesus, and James joined Mary Magdalene, at the tomb carrying sweet spices with the pretense of anointing the body. As was the plan, they would find the tomb empty, but saw the "vision of angels" (Matthew). As the first witness to the empty tomb, Mary Magdalene went to tell Peter and John, (John) and immediately after returned to the tomb. She remained there weeping at the door. According to the New Testament, she was the first witness of the Resurrection appearances of Jesus, though at first, she claimed not to recognize him. When he said her name, she was recalled to consciousness and cried Rabboni, or in English, Teacher.

Let me back up a bit: The earliest societies and religions were matriarchal, kings were sacrificed, and the female moon was thought to control the male sun. The newer world religions were monotheist—Judaism, Islam, and Christianity--with one God who was male, and they took shape in the Iron Age when men dominated societies in Europe and the Middle East. Even then some fathers of the early Christian church argued that women had no souls. Goddess cultures of the past tended to be egalitarian (all are equal), earth-centered, and non-violent.

Ancient Australian Aboriginal rock paintings similarly show the powerful sexuality of women in explicit detail. Naga is a serpent god in India and translates to dragon in Japanese. Many religions feature the dragon or snake representing knowledge, wisdom, and or healing. Then there is the double snake as a supreme goddess, often androgynous (blending of both male and female), capable of creation without a male partner.

The idea of a Holy Trinity did not form part of Israelite theology and only became a Christian concept as the gospel spread into the pagan world, where a holy triad or family was a well-established device. The Holy Spirit or Ghost was female in Hebrew texts.

In early religions some figures show a long phallic head and neck symbolizing that the Great Goddess is both male and female with the power to create all - this Androgynes is found in many religions - Nommo (a fish) in

Mali and Sudan, Africa and also Gaia (Earth) in Greece who gave birth alone to Chronos (Time) and Uranus (Space). In Egypt, the creator god Atum was both male and female, with different manifestations.

Lilith, (Sumerian/Hebrew), Adam's first wife, as is written on the first page of the Old Testament, was desecrated as a warning to all. In Jewish legend, she was a woman demon who had sex with any and all men. In Babylon, she was a child-slaying demon, and it is said that God created her out of the Earth like Adam, but she refused to submit to him and fled. Some stories say she secretly became friends with Eve. Her daughters were the lovers of Cain and Abel, which would clear up the mystery of how the human population grew.

Just lately there seems to be some new physical evidence female Androgynies lived on this Earth for years before the male first appeared.

Back to Mary Magdalene, first and foremost is the relationship that Jesus Christ had with Mary Magdalene, Salome, and his Mother, but especially Mary Magdalene. It is my interpretation that Jesus' true disciples were those three women, and possibly many more. That the exorcism of demons from these women was in actuality a transcendence of their energies from being tainted due to preconditioning to pure. That the positioning of Jesus as the Jewish Messiah was the handiwork of the Essenes, John the Baptist, the male Apostles, and later the founders of the Holy Roman Catholic Church.

I also believe that Jesus discovered the true essences of the female and male and their proper place in the universal order of things. Jesus, having been sent to the East to study by John the Baptist, left there before finishing his education, and returned having honed his paranormal powers far beyond the normal person. These powers were used by the Essenes to convince the Hebrew population of his divinity.

Jesus, somewhere along the way, discovered his ability to create transcendence in the special women that surrounded him. When the Essenes and the Apostles discovered that Jesus believed he had found these abilities, they threatened him, his wife, and mother until he agreed to their plan of a crucifixion where he could use his powers of slowing his heart rate to practically a standstill approximating death. He convinced the women who were his disciples to go along with and take part in the Essenes scheme to save the illusion of him as the Messiah, and in return, they would allow him and his true Apostles safe passage.

I also believe that there are records as yet unfound that prove what I just said to be true. That Jesus transformed both Mary's and Salome beyond the normal female infusing them with pure energy to become In-Perpetuum Beings upon their deaths.

AFTERWORD

Having read this book, you should be aware that it means nothing unto itself. As I have said and/or quoted many times throughout, words are useless in matters of spiritual awakening. True and meaningful wisdom comes from experience and manifesting knowledge in one's life. I have only provided a beginning outline for Pure Mind practice and the philosophical seeds to begin your quest.

You must learn the Truth of your life's purpose through awakening experience and living with a dedicated, faithful practice. The strength of resolve helps evoke spiritual enlightenment and provides the deep inner faith needed to attain the state of perpetual existence. While you are in a meditative state, Universal Nature provides you with the knowledge and understanding of why, who, and what you are through awakening experiences. This may seem to take a very long time, but seriously what better can you do with your lifetime?

The first step and all steps that follow are up to you. I hope that you take the necessary steps to venture inward and in turn are successful in putting to rest your "hungry ghost."